The Original Manuals of Noble Ape

Tom Barbalet

Copyright © 2011 by Tom Barbalet. All rights reserved.

ISBN 978-1-257-50243-1

Originally written 1996-1997.

Cover photographs by Michele Barbalet.

http://www.nobleape.com/

Contents

	Introduction	1
1.	Overview	5
2.	The Land, Existence and Time	11
3.	The Species	28
4.	The Mechanics	34
5.	The Program	43
6.	Sex, Birth, Life and Death	49
7.	I See, Therefore I Am	59
8.	Infinite vs. Identity	71
9.	Creation Information	68
A.	The Uniqueness of Nervana	76
B.	Polymorphic Image Analysis	81
C.	There Exists A Tree	84

Introduction

When the application called 'Nervana' first appeared, the software was very primitive. Had the project relied on the software alone, it would have died a quiet death soon after the release of Nervana 0.1. However, the manual offered some indication of what the program would become, and this hope combined with a certain element of wonder created the three manual tome, 'A Tale of Nervana'. This insured the project remained alive, albeit in a critical condition. The collection of documents where never completed, and remained dormant for the six or so months, just before the final development of the CD/CD-ROM. Nevertheless, with the CD-ROM nearing completion, an edited version of the Tale needed to be created in order to offer the owner of the CD-ROM some indication of the future of the project.

'A Tale of Nervana' existed as some indication that the author of the project had been willing to put in many hours to produce a text that remained allusive and alienating to all but the most persistent reader. Much of the original confused elements in the philosophy of 'A Tale of Nervana', were reworded in some logical but more importantly brief form for 'A Tale of Nervana'. Still much of the original Tale waited to be explained as did the interpolation of the remaining, apparently forever lost sections of the text. These sections dealt with;

- Desire and fear rendering within the Noble Ape identity structure,
- Implementation of the software into education,
- The biology and methods of the fierce feline,
- Evolution and rebellion,
- Some exact definition of the population density framework,
- The command line intelligence interface, and,
- Storage formats and identity files.

These merely represent those ideas that occurred to me on the evening of typing this text. They offer no indication of the hole-ridden nature of documentation for this project. I hope to offer some indication of how to interpolate answers to questions that may not appear to be covered in these texts. I have tried to include all the important and linking sections of the original manuals, as well as the somewhat amusing interludes. It is hard to avoid these actually. The more I edit, the more I realize that rather than editing down the three manuals, I am in fact creating even larger monsters.

The text contained in the Nervana manuals should be considered as a drop in the ocean of the total documentation of the project. I have considered including more supporting texts. It would be tempting to include a large number of polymorphic analysis texts as scribed over the years. This would only lead to more confusion and an explanatory history that would dramatically predate the project even more than the discussion of 1980s action films and DOTMAN movement (which you will find inside). Rather than treating this CDROM as an opportunity to put every manual and novel ever written by me, I have chosen to include only the manuals and texts surrounding the Nervana Project. This has been done for two reasons;

- To give a clear indication of the amount that is yet to be done, and,
- Entice the reader into contacting the author and arguing point for point through the development of the project.

Both points will result in the placement of a Nervana wall through the project's web site where people will be able to offer possible solutions and rewrites to certain aspects of the Nervana manual.

The first point should also be noted in bold CAPITALS.

The manuals offered here are drafts. Please do not feel conned by the idea that you have in fact purchased a set of drafts, a demo game and some wacko sounds. The purchase aids the further development of the project.

It has been noted that ideally, one day, the text shown here should be put into a book: a solid thing with many pages and some illustrations. That the time of writing this digital file, it seems a long way off. Although it would be rather nice to be able to hold the Nervana manuals and other assorted texts in one's hand. Stay tuned for more information.

The documents presented have actually been connected to sections of time when they were written. The exception of this is Nervana Philosophic, which is/was designed to be timeless and a set of lines in the sand. The software referred to has had many forms. The basic all-you-need-to-know version is that the program for the project, the simulation, was originally called Nervana. This became a little confusing when the program expanded to a broader project with the simulation in the center. Thus somewhere over late 1996, the name of the simulation program was changed to Iota that stood for Isle of the Apes. In early 1997, in order to get a development grant from the Australian Film Commission the game, Escape from Nervana was conceived. Rather ironically, the game required a much higher resolution than the previous simulation. So again Iota had to re-morph into something more detailed which complied more strictly with the Nervanian mathematics.

The history of Nervana as presented in the manuals set in aluminum here is quite heavily censored. This has been done for productive personal reasons more than anything. I would much rather have a collection of texts that gave some indication of the possibility of a happy future for the project. Obviously having worked on this project for the better part of a year and a half, there have been many downs, and a few decent ups! My personal feeling is, in order for you to have a CDROM in your computer something needed to go right with this project. I do not want the manuals to act as transcripts to the continuous petty problems of the project.

Having said all of this, I probably should let you read the text. If I have not scared you off. I should note that very few people have actually read the manual from one end to the other. Nevertheless, those who have seem to enjoy it.

This manual explains the construction of the Nervana application. Nervana was designed as a new media project, that is a program that teaches through a hands on exploration of science and philosophy. The virtual reality interface and real-time accessibility to information were secondary effects that stemmed from the use of the infinite virtual reality algorithms that are constructed in this manual. This interface meant that the Nervana application was not a rules based simulation, such as Life or the Sim series from Maxis, but as the name suggests - an infinite virtual reality environment. It is possible through the techniques developed in infinite virtual reality environments to study something as small as ant colonies or something as large as the geomorphology of the island.

This document was originally designed to be a manual, but as time continued it became obvious that a disciplinary categorized manual was inhibiting to a majority of readers who did not hold university-level understanding of the specific fields (of Quantum Mechanics, Metaphysics, Epistemology, Number Theory, Advanced Calculus etc). The information was then developed into a comfortably read text, acceptable for general reading and useful for analysis that is more detailed. Please treat this information like a case-construction sheet, as this is how I have created the manual

All information and discussion is the original thought of Tom Barbalet, unless otherwise stated, and thus subject to copyright. The development of this application will take at least three years. This text is intended to be read for work in progress information.

Tom Barbalet, the creator of Nervana and this manual, is an Arts and Science student at the Australian National University, Canberra, studying Philosophy and Physics. He has written virtual reality engines, anti-viral software, polymorphic compilers and too many games. In his spare time, he writes novels, cycles, listens to records, mixes sounds and meets with friends. His most recent exploits include trying to find some definition in his life, writing lots of low-level C and playing the piano.

Tom Barbalet, December 1997,
Adelaide, South Australia.

Written from June 1996 to December 1997
By Tom Barbalet

1. Overview

On 12 June 1996, there was nothing, just a few ideas of a world of islanders roaming freely over a simple simulation. Then on 13 June 1996, I sent a video to a friend in Malaysia. The video included a section that described a conversation had between myself and a fellow called James Morauta. This was the beginning of Nervana. A project that would take computer simulation further than it had ever been taken before, into the realm of the imagination; past the sensible, past the rational, into the chaotic imagination. The challenge was twofold;

- To create a realistic, sustainable ecosystem within a computer simulation, and,
- To create a reasonable method for sentient beings to exist within this simulation

The first was easily achievable, to a certain extent. The mathematics of sustainable ecosystem would solve itself, but creating an ecosystem that could maintain itself through near-random fluctuations was the problem.

The second challenge was virtually inconceivable. How would such a thing operate and who would it answer to? It had to be impossible. From the realm of creating such a program to the outcomes and use of this program, every step of the way gave another set of infinite questions that appeared to have no answer.

Although the video footage does not reveal much of the scope or power of the project, the initial idea came from a conversation had between Morauta and myself on that cold Canberra winter's morn. As I remember it, we had been debating the fundamental intelligence of machines. There was a problem posed by an academic, if I cared sufficiently I should probably find it and quote it formally. As much of modern philosophy was taught, this belief about the fundamental philosophical dumbness of machines could only be considered plausible if it entered the belief systems of the students that were supposed to study it. Most philosophers, or certainly the academics that surrounded me, refused the possibility that a computer could ever behave like a sentient being or even worse, be able to simulate the interactions of sentient beings.

Perhaps from our very beginnings entering a society of ever-increasing technology, we are taught to acknowledge the differences between humans and all other objects in the universe. This causes us particular problems when wondering what happens to humans after they no longer show the signs humanity. I look at this division argument with considerable skepticism. If there is one defining sign of humanity it is our ability to utilize tools. What good is a simulation like Nervana? I became bogged in the meta-problems of the mere concept of Nervana before I had even begun. Everywhere I turned, people were willing to assist with sections of the simulation, up until a point; up until the simulation appeared to be too smart. The initial development of ideas could really be seen up until about December 1996. By this time, a rather cute Mac application was floating the internet. It featured a small tribe of Noble Apes wandering an island. It's development occurred with no real publicity. Nevertheless, returning to the early development, it came through a lot of first principle pondering.

The claim of the first paragraph that this project takes simulation further than it has been taken before causes many to discount this text and the project before reading any further. I think personally that the rich contextual nature of the project leads one somewhat closer to the desired outcome. It can be interpreted by the reader as a purely arrogant claim, but I wish to add that to my knowledge the holistic way the project approaches the issues of (i) and (ii) are in combination would appear to be unique. I do not have all the answers about a complete simulation that offers all that is described in this text. However, it would appear that I have found something along my wanderings. The lack of connective communication, resulting in many new and wonderful wheels being created in research and development phases of the project, makes me wonder if there are not a few Nervanas already existing out there.

I would like to issue a challenge to skeptics of the project. See if you can read the remainder of these Nervana Manuals. This is challenge enough for the non-skeptic! If you come to the end of the manuals, and still doubt the project's viability, consider yourself a true skeptic. The arguments entered into here are not sophist arguments. In fact, these documents could be more comfortably described as a working notebook that I have used while developing the project.

The first indication that the electronic community had of the project came when I emailed Doug Rushkoff, author of Cyberia: In the Trenches of Hyperspace and Mediavirus, with my frustrations with the project and the publicity it would not receive, it was early June 1996. I could not expect to fund such a project by myself. I was 19 at the time and had some small savings from working in a Research School on campus: not enough to buy even one new compiler and a new computer. Rather than become bogged down with the problems of 10 year old technology, I turned to developing as much of the software as physically possible. I travelled to Malaysia and while there released the first version of the Nervana application. It was described in a large post on 19 July 1996;

'While up here [in Malaysia] I have been pulling together a dare-application. Like many of my recent bits of code, this one came up in conversation with my friend James K. Morauta, a Philosophy student in his Honors Year at ANU, about simulating human desires in a computer. He said it could not be done, I said it could, and the rest is Nervana.

'Nervana simulates an island, with a small population of 'Noble Apes'. The program simulates everything on the island, from insects to thunder storms, using a number of simple and realistic algorithms.'

It was later described in the original Nervana manual as 'a tribal village simulator which was designed after a discussion with a fellow called James Morauta about the extent to which computer simulation could be used to describe things such as human desires.'

I had begun trying to simulate the motion of humanoids with some of my early virtual reality applications. Although I liked creating natural virtual landscapes without the intrusion of humans, eventually I wanted to add some 'villagers' to travel across the land to fish, hunt and gather. The motion of these 'villagers' was based on my DOTMAN movement.

The four rules of DOTMAN movement;

if $current\_x > desired\_x$ then
$\quad current\_x = current\_x - 1$
if $current\_y > desired\_y$ then
$\quad current\_y = current\_y - 1$
if $current\_x < desired\_x$ then
$\quad current\_x = current\_x + 1$
if $current\_y < desired\_y$ then
$\quad current\_y = current\_y + 1$

What this says in non-technical language is that the current point moves one unit closer to the desired point in the x and y direction. This produced a diagonal and straight approach for the 'villagers' to find their way around. The creation of this very basic follower logic came through some very early software I wrote when I was thirteen or fourteen. It was originally called predator logic, which came from a lot of pondering having watched the action movie, the Predator. It was at a time when I had just written a vector landscape UFO simulator. This game was the basis for all my later vector programs. The UFO simulator had two types of predators, stationary ground-bases and enemy UFOs. The central theme in the film that I wanted to include in the game was a sense of being watched and stalked by a virtually unstoppable predator. This emotion was also fundamental in the development of Escape from Nervana. The sense of being stalked that a Noble Ape should feel is central to the success of the game. If this feeling is not conveyed to the user, to the point where the user almost feels as the ape feels, then the game has failed. The player should also be aware that they are opposed by a great and equally matched foe. This would appear to be different to most games where the objective is to allow the user to gain ground and not be forced to train to play the game!

Returning to my discussion of primitive movement algorithms explored. Through developing more detailed virtual reality environments came the FAMILIAR movement, which looked for paths holding roughly the same height. This contour hugging movement looked more realistic for any viewer of the environment, but still failed to create any simulation of reality. It was with this frustration that I decided to create the Nervana simulation. The most important part of the application was the creation of desires for the Noble Apes (occasionally referred to as NAs) to have. These desires motivate the NAs to move. This method of movement is pure in its form. The created creatures are not obeying some static series of rules that simulate movement that appears to be realistic. The NAs in the simulation are actually moving though desire-driven motivation. This took some serious thought and experimentation.

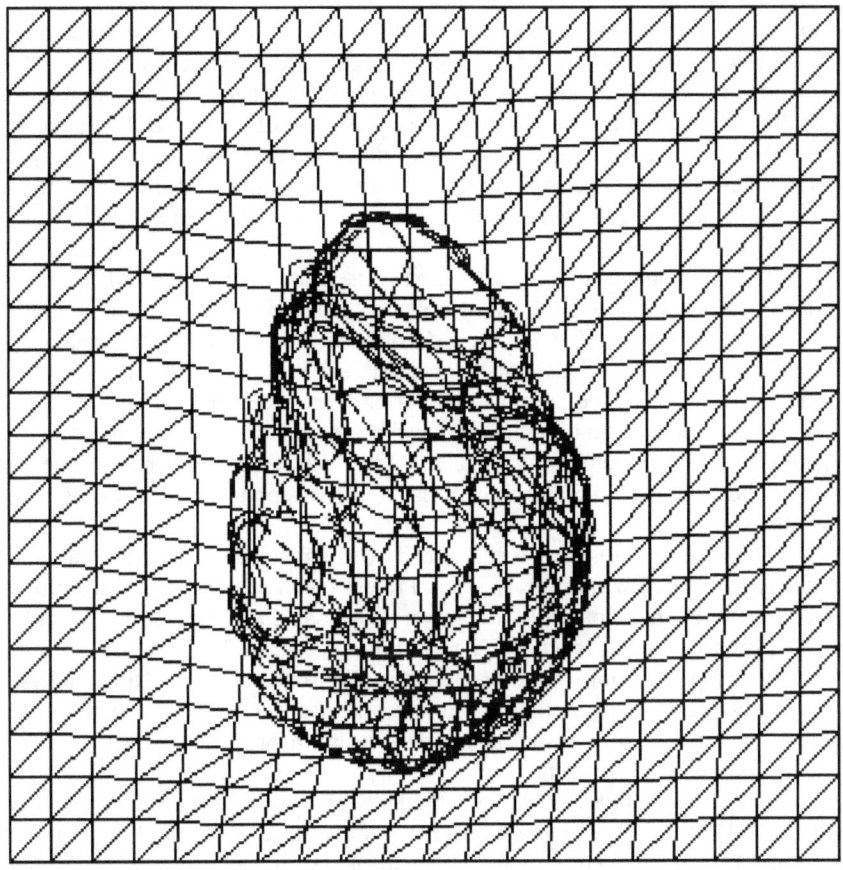

Image of a Noble Ape's path over an island (test image August 1996)

An interesting aspect of the Nervana Project is that it has brought together many different disciplines - albeit in a gradual sense. I have had to educate myself in many other fields while completing a Physics and Philosophy degree. The implementation of fuzzy logic systems (and the removal of fuzzy logic systems), quantum mechanics and complexity-based polymorphic systems (which replaced the fuzzy logic systems) within a tight programming framework has challenged me as a programmer and a thinker. This became even more self-evident in the development of Escape from Nervana or more importantly the Psi infinite virtual reality engine. Here it became a question of developing something that visually modeled nature at an alarming speed.

As you may have gathered, in this document I hope to describe how the application was created and the theories that were implemented in order to make the Nervana Project a reality. I am not going to 'dumb-down' any of the information. This documentation may prove hard going. I will try to avoid lapses into computer and physics based terminology in order to describe how the program does certain things, but I will try to keep all the meta-theory in coherent language. Having said this, many readers have found this text hard going. In a more ideal, caring world, I would employ someone to rewrite these monstrous tomes into something that could be enjoyed by all. Nevertheless, somewhat paradoxically, I guess in a more ideal, caring world, I would be sufficiently well centered as to not have continued with the project past its initial design phase.

The importance of this application rests in its ability to simulate. The first question one must ask when one uses Nervana is why? What are we as a programmer or a user trying to see or achieve? The most obvious point I would like to make is that Nervana is a simulation. I do not believe for one instant that the purpose of this application is to play God, nor is it to offer some deep insight into any of the disciplines that the Nervana application touches upon. Really when I am asked what the purpose of this program is, I have to say that it is just a game. A huge game really: a dare application and nothing more. What this dare-application can be used for is more interesting.

The application is very well defined in its structure. There is no way that the technology developed within the Nervana Project could be used in a word processor for example. It is, thus not really a commercially viable application. So where is it's market? Bored University students? I would argue that the Nervana application is a tool - a philosophical tool - or perhaps just a philosophical game. Nevertheless, the purpose of the game is to simulate a population of near-humans on a small island and to offer a validity test of a desire theory. The desire theory being similar to Russell's arguments on Logical Atomism.

The strange problem was my thoughts on Logical Atomism soon became clouded in Glandular Fever that affected me from late August to late December 1996. This period is characterized by many hours spent sleeping and the remaining waking ones spent coding the project and writing the manual (most of which is still nestled in these many kilobytes.) It is hard to say what was actually developed over this period. The Glandular Fever robbed me of some of my memory surrounding this period. The main memory is that this period of sickness was a catch-up period of writing much of the documentation that I had previously theorized.

The early ideas of desires and a fear look-up table came to me over this period. My main memory comes of sitting up in bed in my College room on campus.

Feeling sick and tired, but typing away trying to get all my ideas down. It soon became obvious that almost all I wanted to write would never make it to paper in any intelligible form. When this thought entered my mind, I would always begin coding as a means to stall my discontent with documentation.

Recovering, I travelled to Adelaide from Canberra, and spent some time with the Mindflux/inSect collective. Much time was spent running Nervana and discussing the theory of objects and the way objects filtered into the identity and in particular, desire structures through the identity. Over this time, I started theorizing the visual mapping into the identity. Here space, and time through motion, is mathematically carved into the identity. This carving process also defined distinct objects that could belong to sets of objects and hold uniqueness. With the mathematical documentation of this written in part, I began work writing an intelligent database/thesaurus management tool. It was very separate from my work with Nervana, and it helped to pay for the CD I was to press at the end of 1997.

I spoke to Nik of inSect about ways to get better computer equipment to write the simulation on; he recommended I approach the Australian Film Commission for a grant. This process took about five months to get. Over which time, I concentrated mainly on documentation, perhaps partially due to the anticipatory nature of the new computer, but also because the existing software was heavily optimized.

Receiving the grant from the Australian Film Commission, I began work on the Psi virtual reality engine. Due to University and various dead-end research and development trails, five months later a fast landscape engine was developed with a lot of CD audio. This period was a section of great motivational change. Prior to this time, the project had been a thing of curiosity for me. I was interested in testing the boundaries and seeing what I could see. Nevertheless, over this time, I actually realized that in order for the project to survive, I had to think of ways of it touching more people. The CD audio was the best way to communicate. Although the printed word had existed many generations before the audio CD, it amused me, that now the audio CD was a more popular format for mass communication.

The motivation change for me came in a sense that I had already achieved something, somewhere along the path towards the conclusion of the project. The project stopped being something I was curious about and became something I was developing. This movement rested uneasy.

Little programming or documentation work was done over this time towards the old Nervana program. Now known as Iota: Isle of the Apes. The grant had originally been requested for the development of the whole project. Soon it was only used for the development of Psi. Some programming for Iota was done at the time just before the CD/CDROM release, and similarly the documentation was expanded. However, this was only done as a panicking afterthought and not something with any productive value.

2. The Land, Existence and Time

The majority of the meta-philosophy of the project was inspired by the eighth lecture of Bertrand Russell in Gordon Square, London, in 'the first months of 1918'; 'Excursus into Metaphysics: What There Is'. These lectures are known collectively 'The Philosophy of Logical Atomism'. For the record, I came to these lectures well after beginning my arguments and programming. The total agreement of this lecture with my approach to the Nervana application made me feel that this simulation would not only be possible but also a plausible means of simulating a rational desire creation theory.

When I wrote the initial movement generators for the NAs, I was able to create secondary results from primary systems. By instructing each ape to look forward and turn to the right if they 'saw' water ahead, many apes learnt to override this 'rule' and experiment with swimming. These apes also went on to not fear water. The apes that did not have the fear of water would not panic when the user moved the apes into even the deepest water.

To summarize, and probably oversimplify, Russell's theory, everything that is described by metaphysics - wants, desires, identity etc - can in fact be described by 'sense data' collected over time. Unfortunately, this collection over time can only be done at the minimum 'dt' interval of one minute. Thus, the program has been modified to accommodate such a large time interval. It should be noted that the concepts of identity, desires and fear etc, come from this point and merely describe the Logi-atomic bundles of sense-data in a more computable and conceptually viable form. This may appear to be a cop out, and as I am writing around the text, I find it very difficult to explain concisely how the final concoction of philosophy that makes Nervana Philosophic for example can really be equated with Russellian thought. It should be noted that this claim was made early in the project, although I will conclude by noting that if one considers all the forms in Nervana Philosophic to be latent, then one gets Logical Atomism.

This is really the briefest introduction to the philosophy of the project. Nevertheless, it is all I will enter to here. If you feel somewhat shortchanged, my recommendation is that you read Nervana Philosophic now. The detailed discussions featured and somewhat self-satirized later in this continuing text, was the flabby framework from which Nervana Philosophic was built. The interesting point comes when the methods of processing have been sufficiently described linguistically and the remaining work can only be done through mathematics. This linking ultimately between conceptual philosophical principles and raw applicative mathematics is a real of exploration that may be out of reach for this text. Although detailed segments are offered. I now must return to the primary details of the program.

Nervana's clock has four hands. The first two central hands tell 12-hour time. The user should be able to work out if it is AM or PM by the sun. The hand to the right is the 'month' hand. Nervana operates on thirteen 28-day lunar months - a 364-day year. One full rotation equals a 28-day month. The hand to the left is the 'year' hand. One full rotation equals a 364-day year. The seasons can be found by seeing the left-hand travel through quarter-rotations. Each season is roughly 91 days.

The whole system of rainfall, sun-levels and dawn/dusk-times are calculated with probability based on seasonal times. This is done by fitting the year to a sine wave traveling through 2-pi. This wave is then 'fuzzied' by adding plus/minus ~60% of the maximum.

Thus, the weather variable recalculated each hour is equal to;

$w = s + r$

Where s is the seasonal-sine variable ranging from -840 to 840 and r is the random fuzzy variable ranging from -500 to 500.

The logic in this version says that the three states;

NOTHING (840 up)
CLOUDY
RAINING (-840 down)

Can exist in both day and night to the same probability, the NOTHING state is in fact just a sunny day or a star-filled night. The chance of a change in conditions is dependent on the length of time that each state is held for. It is not likely that it will rain for just 10 minutes (except for isolated 'Spring Showers'). Moreover, it is improbable to cycle from raining to cloudy to sunny to cloudy to raining to sunny in an hour. (Un)fortunately having lived in both Canberra, Australia and Kuala Lumpur, Malaysia, I am familiar with quite dramatic changes of weather, and it may be argued that there need not exist a transition of cloudiness at all. However, for the time being, I will use the hour variation method in Nervana.

The initial programming of the application was just to draw a realistic model of an island. There a few interesting quirks with the island creation which I should probably describe early in the piece. The land creation in Nervana allows for an infinite resolution, hence the idea of 'infinite virtual reality'. This infinite resolution is created through the multiplication of two sine-Fourier series, one representing the x-axis and one representing the y-axis.

The land is formed with the 'modeling' of ten genetic variables, each ranging from -8 to 8. In order to explain what variables are produced we need to define the back-slash-division operator as follows;

$a = x \setminus y$

for $y \diamond 0$, $a=x/y$; for $y=0$, $a=0$.

One must also define the array 'gen' from one to ten, and the array sd which is an integer sine generator with an amplitude of 840, and a resolution of 256 over 2-pi. x and y are integers ranging from 0 to 128.

f(x) = sd[x] + sd[2*x]\(4*gen[1]) + sd[3*x]\(4*gen[2]) + sd[4*x]\(4*gen[3]) + sd[5*x]\(4*gen[4]) + sd[6*x]\(4*gen[5])
g(y) = sd[y] + sd[2*y]\(4*gen[6]) + sd[3*y]\(4*gen[7]) + sd[4*y]\(4*gen[8]) + sd[5*y]\(4*gen[9]) + sd[6*y]\(4*gen[10])
z(x,y) = ((f(x)/7)*(g(y)/7))/450

This formula comes from the original Nervana program. With the introduction of the PowerMac's PowerPC processor a lot more resolution was added in both the normal and the planer quantization. Most of the text below is included for historical reasons. The new Iota program does most of the 'modes' all on screen at once. In this old Nervana standard the water-level is defined at z(x,y)=10. Each z unit equals 10 meters and each contour bar in CONTOUR/APE mode represents a change of 100m.

Other than the practical realities of land formation, one must wonder how things such as trees are put into the simulation. From a philosophical stand-point the placing of trees, rocks, beaches and bushes in the simulation is as important as giving the NA life. In order for the NA to collect sense data and an understanding of their reality, they must have some sense of location. Thus, the most important point of placing a tree in the Nervana landscape is that it will be determined as a unique entity. This may seem like a fictitious creation. When is a tree ever planted to make a scene appear to be unique? Being a precocious oregano grower I will answer, when is a tree ever planted to make a scene appear to be the same? This is unfortunately a case were one as a programmer must make certain allowances for the poor resolution of the simulation. The NA does not operate on a 25m resolution; it operates at a 0.25m resolution! One must write in the unique locations of objects to reduce the NAs' reliance on poor resolution and the identification of gradients.

In this version of Nervana, the island (including the surrounding water) is divided into 128 by 128 squares. The island and water as shown in the simulation is 3200m by 3200m. Thus, the land resolution of the island is 25m. The movement of the NAs is divided a further 100 times, giving their movement a resolution of 0.25m. The land resolution can be seen in the CONTOUR/APE mode, each square 'pixel' represents a single land-square. In the VECTOR mode, each square represents a square of 100m by 100m (a hectare).

The three calculus items (delta z/delta x, delta z/delta y and del z) are just mathematical descriptions of the land. Moreover, the Operators were added to the program at a testing level and remained as a beautiful addition. The del z graph might be considered practical as it describes the fastest possible route down the slope - in lay terms. The mathematically astute will notice it is in fact a map of negative del z. Positive del z is less informative.

The land creation section of the program is not designed to offer any realistic information or even be moderately factual! The process just offers a good and quickly generated palette with which to add things like trees and bushes. The simple fact that the program creates an island with a beautiful square zeroing somewhere out to sea shows that this is a limiting factor in the simulation. When the program is adapted to a more powerful system, this simplification of a Fourier system will be removed.

The Contour/Ape mode displays the NA roaming free, and the Observe/Control mode enables the user to gain a more detailed look at each individual NA as well as the ability to control them.

The landscape in the Nervana simulation needs to have two properties - uniqueness and compactness. The property of uniqueness comes from the intertwined idea of existence through external stimuli. This is expanded in a more simplified form in Appendix C. In order for the NA on the island to generate an idea of self, they must have an idea of their location on the island. This comes though roaming the island and observing unique features of various sections of the island. It would not be sensible for the NA to find a valley on the island that was identical to another valley on the island. Plausibly, although this is seriously brought into question through Appendix A, there could exist a point on the island that was identical to another point on the island through its surroundings. The positioning of features on the island is crucial in stopping a loss of uniqueness through poor resolution. It is implausible for there to exist two identical places in our reality that are identical - at least with our eyes open.

The second requirement for a simulation of this size and structure is the requirement of compactness. This is important particularly when one takes into account the size of the simulation in physical space and the number of trees that could exist on such islands. For this reason, a quantum modeling system has been developed to show the greater information of each island generated by the simulation. Speed is an important requirement of the simulation and keeping a database record of the progression of every tree on the island would be quite a task.

Before going on, it is important to note the information that the program generates with each island. Ideally, the only information the simulation would store would be the Fourier genetics of the island, but practically the island has to be mapped quickly and thus the f, g, df and dg are all generated to a resolution of 25m. From this the land description is taken by;

$$z(x,y) = f(x) * g(y)$$
$$\partial x(x,y) = df(x) * g(y)$$
$$\partial y(x,y) = f(x) * dg(y)$$

In order to simulate biological principles, important factors need to be formulated. These factors are called operators. This term comes from quantum mechanics and it just describes a formula that can be created from the initial land-description.

H - height
A - area
W - water
O - moving sunlight
U - sunlight

The important information is the way that these operators are constructed to be normalized and positive. For the operators to be normalized means that if one added all the points together of one operator it would equal that of all the points of any other operator. This is not technically what normalizability means in mathematics or quantum mechanics but it has a purpose in the definition that shall be used here.

Water and moving sunlight are Boolean operators, thus they can only be true or false, but as a numerical value must be assigned to every operator, a result of false meaning water or no sunlight at that time, and that point respectively results in a value of zero for the operator. This is slightly against the spirit of infinite virtual reality, but it is done in the initial stages of the simulation. This shall be removed as the program moves onto a more advanced system.

In the early versions of Nervana, all operators are shown at a resolution of 100m. This is a huge resolution for such information to be described with - but in order to test out the very basics of the application this resolution was used. This gives 32 x 32 points. As a reasonable standard, assume that the operators average to 16 per point over the 3.2 x 3.2 km grid. This 16 represents an abstract value or a height of the graph at that point. 16384 points per grid with the 32 x 32 grid.

Appendix A shows a formal mathematical account of the uniqueness of any location on the island. The importance of the derivative is purely in the slope of the surface on which an object (tree, rock, bush etc) is put. This position must be considered unique in the landscape in order to be seen as a marker for the NA. Our analysis thus far show us that unless the genetic land information for f(x) and the genetic land information for g(y) are equal (i.e. (x)((f(x)=g(x))(df(x) = dg(x))) then the slope of the land for any possible location will be unique at any location, viewed from any direction. This is a important conclusion, but in terms of what it means to a creature that can view the island it is small. A far more important analysis is the uniqueness of the objects themselves. Before this is elaborated, we should construct the factors that make general biological systems.

These factor are described in a simple table, showing how the sub-operators are connected, the system needs to be simplified to the initial operators. Here an important problem of biological simulation is raised. Let us take the R (rock) sub operator; it has a formation from A and ~T. What this says is that you will find a rock where the area (or slope) is great and where there are no trees. The T sub operator is formed from the initial operators W U A H, or water, sunlight, area and height. Just through simple thought processes, it seems obvious that water and sunlight should have little to do with the position of a rock on the island. Thus in the table below the initial operators are simplified to A and ~H. The '~' or '-' refers to a subtraction of the initial operators instead of and addition, thus it is possible to have a negative value for a point on the graph of a sub-operator.

Op	Object Group
W	*Water*
H	*Height*
A	*Area*
U	*Sunlight*
O	*Moving Sunlight*
C	*Beach*
R	*Rocks* (Rocks A, B, C and D)
G	*Grasses* (Grasses A and B)
B	*Bushes (general)* (Berry, Bean, Fruit and Nut Bushes)
P	*Potato Plant*
F	*Flowering Bushes* (Flowering Bushes A and B)
T	*Trees* (Boat Wood and Non-Descriptive Trees A, B and C)
L	*Fungi*
I	*Insects* (Ant, Spider and Fly)
S	*Sea-Fish*
M	*Mice* (Insectivorous and Herbivorous Mice)
E	*Sea-Bird*
N	*Night-Bird*
D	*Seed-Eating Bird*
V	*Insectivorous Bird*

Op	Object Group	Formed By
A	Area	initial operator
B	Bushes (general)	W U A H
C	Beach	~A ~R ~H
D	Seed-Eating Bird	B G
E	Sea-Bird	S T
F	Flowering Bushes	W U A
G	Grasses	U A ~T ~B ~F
H	Height	initial operator
I	Insects	W A ~O
L	Fungi	W R U
M	Mice	W A H ~O
N	Night-Bird	M ~O
O	Moving Sunlight	initial operator
P	Potato	W U
R	Rocks	A ~T
S	Sea-Fish	~W ~H
T	Trees	W U A H
U	Sunlight	initial operator
V	Insectivorous Bird	I T B
W	Water	initial operator

Final Result

	W	U	A	H	O
B	+	+	+	−	.
C	.	.	−	+	.
D	+	+	+	−	.
E	.	+	+	.	.
F	+	+	+	.	.
G	.	+	+	−	.
I	+	.	+	.	−
L	+	+	+	+	.
M	+	.	+	+	−
N	.	.	+	+	−
P	+	+	.	.	.
R	.	.	+	−	.
S	−	.	.	−	.
T	+	+	+	+	.
V	+	+	+	.	−

W - 2 bits   U - 1 bit   A - 2 bit
H - 2 bits   O - 1 bits   8 bits total

Now we have this idea of normalized positive initial operators, let us define H and A;

$H(x,y) = z(x,y) * z(x,y)$
$A(x,y) = \partial x(x,y) * \partial x(x,y) + \partial y(x,y) * \partial y(x,y)$

The W operator is defined as;

0 where there is water, and,
16384/(number of points without water) where there is no water.

The U operator is defined as;

0 where there is no sunlight at a that time, and,
16384/(number of points with sunlight at that time) where there is sunlight at that time.

The O operator is defined as the combination of all the sunlight over a period of a day at any given point on the grid.

Please note that W and U are described normalized, the remaining initial operators are normalized as a secondary process.

Once this process has been followed on all the sub-operators, a population factor can be attributed to each individual species on the island. What this factor represents is a level cut through the sub operator's graph. For example, let us say that the fictitious Z sub operator has the following values;

Point	Value
A	-3
B	6
C	10
D	7

Now let us say that within this sub-operator there exists three population factors; 2, 7 and 16. If you look at the original sub-operator translation table, many sub-operators actually feature multiple species types. Simply by dividing the value for the point by the population factor one can gain an indication of the number of that species existing in that location. This translates to;

Point	Value	PF2	PF7	PF16
A	-3	0	0	0
B	6	3	0	0
C	10	5	1	0
D	7	3	1	0

The population factor describes the whole ecosystem of the island and it explains the buffering conditions. It should not be confused with the operators of the island. A good analogy of the two is that the operators provide the mould for the population that fills the mould like water.

The populations need to obey simple laws, all of which are based on the predator/prey matrix;

	B_p	F_p	G_p	L_p	P_p	D_p	E_p	I_p	M_p	N_p	S_p	V_p
B_p	?	0	0	0	0	?	?	?	?	?	?	?
F_p	0	?	0	0	0	?	?	?	?	?	?	?
G_p	0	0	?	0	0	?	?	?	?	?	?	?
L_p	0	0	0	?	0	?	?	?	?	?	?	?
P_p	0	0	0	0	?	?	?	?	?	?	?	?
D_p	0	0	0	0	0	?	?	?	?	?	?	?
E_p	0	0	0	0	0	?	?	?	?	?	?	?
I_p	0	0	0	0	0	?	?	?	?	?	?	?
M_p	0	0	0	0	0	?	?	?	?	?	?	?
N_p	0	0	0	0	0	?	?	?	?	?	?	?
S_p	0	0	0	0	0	?	?	?	?	?	?	?
V_p	0	0	0	0	0	?	?	?	?	?	?	?

$$P_{n+1} = MP_n \text{ where, } P_n = \begin{pmatrix} Bp \\ Fp \\ Gp \\ Lp \\ Pp \\ Dp \\ Ep \\ Ip \\ Mp \\ Np \\ Sp \\ Vp \end{pmatrix}$$

This matrix can be simplified for easier analysis to the simple case;

	Eats	
	Plants	Animals
Plants	p	n
Animals	0	g+s

Before one goes on to describe the four new matrices as defined, one should look at the 'physics' of the simplification. This matrix simplification is designed to aid finding the solution to the inverted version of M. One must find the inverted M in order to say that populations of all the species simulated in this method will maintain themselves. It is important to acknowledge that the equation to calculate the new P is taken once a day and is dependent on another variable, the date during the year. Many creatures and plants on the island are hardwired to give birth or seed at particular times during the year, thus some of the new matrices also have a time component.

p is the plant population growth matrix. It is a 5-square matrix with the diagonal equal to 0. Identifying that plants (initially at least) do not eat other plants. This p matrix must gain its values through a function of time, as the seasonal changes effect plant population and growth. Thus, p will from now on be written as p(t) to show its time dependence.

As plants do not eat animals this section of the matrix M remains all zeros.

n is the description of the animals' consumption of the plants on the island. It is a 7-by-5 matrix.

g is the animal population growth matrix. It is a 7-square matrix with the diagonal equal to 0. It is dependent on the time of the year, and thus, will now be written as g(t) to identify this time dependence.

s is the description of the animal-animal prey on the island. It, like g(t), is a 7-square matrix. This matrix can include cannibalism within the same species and thus the diagonal points can be non-zero.

$$M = \begin{pmatrix} p(t) & n \\ 0 & g(t)+s \end{pmatrix}$$

Ideally what one is trying to achieve with this matrix notation is a situation where;

$$I = \sum_{n=1}^{364} M(n)$$

I.e. after one year, the population maintains itself. The first question one must ask is how much does time perturb p(t) and g(t)? It should be assumed that these factors increase with the same magnitude and under the same shape - hence a concept like the abundance of spring for example. For the early understanding, one can say that time does not play an important role in the simulation and ignore the functionality based on time. Thus;

$$p = p(t)$$
$$g = g(t)$$

This may appear like one step forwards, followed by two steps backwards, but please be reassured that this simplification is useful for some primitive understanding of the system.

I shall use a reduced row echelon inversion method to invert M. Such methods can be frowned upon in terms of slow computation, but I will show some simplifications that do not reduce the resolution of the results. It is important to note that the inverted answer MUST be exact in order for the simulated system to remain stable. I am assuming that this is a very first-year mathematics method of simulating and maintaining a created ecosystem. I hope that this analysis does offer some insight into the project.

The reduced row echelon inversion method should be explained in detail in a good basic linear algebra text. It is done by most main-stream year 11 mathematics students in Australia. I am not sure about the rest of the world. The process is simple. One starts out in this case with a 13x26 matrix. In the first half of the matrix one places M and in the other half one places the identity matrix I. Through a reduction process one moves from;

$$(M \mid I) \text{ to } \quad (I \mid M^{-1})$$

The process is relatively straight-forward particularly with the simplification of p to I. The next question one must ask is how stable is the system created through M? The story does not just end with a comfortable 'I' value after 364 multiplications. The system also needs to remain stable with the felines and the apes roaming and grazing. This requires a very stable if not increasing population on the island. These fluctuations even in the thirteen points case can only be explained through extensive simulation work. I fear that even getting this far in the documentation of the matrix mechanics is alienating for all but the most hardened technical readers. There are four main points to remember in the stability;

- Self maintaining (over a long time),
- Able to stand shock transition (over a short time),
- Break trends of population explosion and implosion, and,
- Offer time explained population growth throughout the year and over years.

The discussion of matrix algebra explains how the macro-ecosystem is created in a relative way. However, it still does not offer an insight into the micro-ecosystem and how the biological system influences the identities of the individual apes on the island. The macro-ecosystem is far easier to describe than the creation of identity for each ape. The remaining section of the manual deals with the creation of identity, the description of the creatures on the island and a little bit of information about the computer program.

Let us continue by asking the initial question. What does the NA 'see' specifically and how is this used to form their identities? The Noble Ape is born helpless; it cannot see and must be protected and nurtured by its mother. Over this period of time the desire structure does not remain dormant. The NA develops a known signature that is the mother. Slowly as the NA gains vision it begins to map out its own perception of the island. This mapping is not in terms of gradient changes, but through shoreline, rocks and trees. The simulation creates such things and places them into a Sketchbook file. This file describes the shoreline, tree and rock structures to a resolution of a meter. It is not assumed that a well travelled NA will be able to intimately know the island to a resolution of a meter. The NA memory can be described briefly with the following diagram;

Location	Outside world	-----------	NA's Brain-----------
Information	Clear	--------> Fuzz ------>	Compressed
Time	--------Instantaneous----------		Later

The Noble Apes are primarily creatures of sight. This is where the first divorce from reality occurs. The simulation can only really begin to describe the collection of vision sense data. Sense data such as touch is almost impossible to simulate realistically with the resolution of the Nervana application. Their vision is described in Chapter 7 in detail. Although the pattern of simplification and modification should be understood early in the reading of this text and it also touches upon simple polymorphic theory.

The NA can feel pain and though the four states of irritation in the system;

Sick
Seriously Sick
Injured
Seriously Injured

It is important to note that injury is an external and sickness is an internal parameter of this application. Although it would be wonderful to simulate the germ-life on the island as well as the viruses, I will try to approximate the spread of disease through NA-to-NA contact. If an NA is generally weak then they will be far more likely to get Sick, and if they do not rest then it will progress into Seriously Sick. It is impossible for an Injured NA to become Seriously Injured through neglect - it must occur through some real interaction with the external world.

Polymorphic Desire Structure - An Introduction before Vision

There are a number of problems in writing the meta-theory that governs any creature's behavior. The creature is born with no eternal knowledge, and slowly develops a sense of identity (internal) and a sense of survival (external). This analysis will not initially allow for societal interaction, but just a roaming Noble Ape (for the time being).

The information, which is described by simple vector co-ordinates in the simulation are mapped onto the NA's brain with a dynamic structure. The ideal scenario for the simulation is that it will be unnecessary to model the exact scenery the NA sees. Nevertheless, can all this information channel into some notion of identity, this is really one of the fundamental questions of the Nervana simulation. There has been an added philosophical complexity added to the simulation by a single email.

Date: Sat, 19 Oct 1996 16:31:49 +0000
From: Bo Daley
To: Thomas Barbalet

evening Tom,

On Fri, 18 Oct 1996, Thomas Barbalet wrote:

> > family an active intervention on your part, or was it a product of
> > the evolutionary process on the island?), how would you describe
> > these constraints?
>
> Reproduction will bring with it genetic family ties which are also
> introduced in the apes conscious. There is a section in BIOLOGY I
> think on that. Not really sure... But there should be. The idea is
> that from very simple ideas like water and mother, the apes develop
> identities and the key thing which divides the apes in the current
> application is;
>
> SEX
> DIRECTION FACING
> LOCATION

yes I remember your analysis of desire as being based on a sort of radical empiricism, in which consciousness is produced by a relation to actual things in the world. While this is certainly a contentious point, it's one that kind of appeals to me, as long as it includes the domain of society and history (i.e. as long as it is not _merely_ the simple ideas of water and mother which determine identity, but also a complex web of social and institutional forces acting upon the body of the subject - this must occur from the moment one allows even the most primitive of institutions into the equation, e.g. the clan, family, village).

Althusser's idea of identity is similar to this point that I'm proposing here - he argues that consciousness is produced by _practice_, which is in turn produced by an institutional relationship to other subjects. In other words, the domain of the social must be accounted for as not merely being part of the sphere of the real, but as _constituting_ in some sense the real, actual things in the world. (i.e. bringing an account of the social back into the empiricist subject).

For this to occur, perhaps I should suggest some ways of dealing with the social dimensions of subjectivity - of course, I don't understand your program enough to be able to assert this with any confidence... that being the case, I wouldn't be surprised if it's just incompatible with your project.. but anyway, here goes: apart from keeping account of each individual NA, perhaps your application should simultaneously be able to keep track of the _normal_ NA (i.e. one that does not exist, but which constitutes the social norm to which all the NAs must relate in some way). Here, Foucault's analysis of the process of subjectivation is helpful. F. argues that discourse in the human sciences does more than simply give an account of the subject; it actually _contributes_ to the formation of subjectivities. For example, the discipline of criminology provides us not merely with a description of the delinquent, but also with an institutional practice to _correct_ these people, to bring them back to a describable conception of the _normal_ individual. Of course, we don't need a complicated scientific discourse like criminology to see the process of normalization in action. All we need is interaction between subjects, and the development of a system of values and morality. Then we begin to see certain aspects of the subject being valorized as 'good' and others as 'bad'. Implicit in such moral determinations is some understanding of what the individual should aspire to be, a model of the subject which is characterized by its moral purity. In this way it would be possible to see the formation of practices in the society of the NAs which have as their intention the normalization of the subject.

What Bo is explaining here is a method of society synthesis. The idea of a mean NA or perhaps a mean NA for every 'x' apes. I remember in perhaps my fifth or sixth year of school I was asked to write a report on government that argued that for every person-per-representative showed an increased disconnection from representation. This could be argued with the construction of a mean NA or a series of mean NAs is a computational comparative nightmare. What I am trying to do here is offer some kind of numerical analysis for the representation or effective representation of the mean NA and how they can motivate and change the NA society. In addition, can we argue that a society can exist in a small population of NA, on the island?

Through development of the ape vs. cat problem which should be discussed in the physics of the simulation, this idea of the mean ape to speed up the pace of the simulation. This mean or average ape, are explicitly used in group movement. Where the group may be facing in many different directions, but the final outcome is a movement in one direction by the group.

The initial philosophical principle of the simulation can be explained through the statement that;

Every subject's desire can be explained through analysis of past history of the subject.

Playing Devil's advocate here, I will offer two possible problems with this hypothesis.

- The subject's desires are considerably more random that this statement allows
- The desires of a person can be back created, but this is not informative of the future

The first problem rests in the notion of random fluctuations effecting existence. Of course, the external world presents problems that cannot be predicted or factored into any possibility of a self contained future. This is not what the initial principle is saying. What it says is at any time a desire structure can be gained by referring to previous identity or memories. Now one may wonder if this is a sensible claim. Obviously, there are certain desires that are close to random and could never really have any connection to previous experience. In reality, this may be the case, but in the case of a simulation such as Nervana, it will be assumed that these random desires are zero summed. That is one random desire at one time will negate another at another time. This may appear to be problematic. What desire functions like a number? What desire could be considered to add to another desire to give a result of zero? It appears to be a very abstract claim. This is not what I am trying to say. Although it appears to be a very abstract claim, what I am saying is that these random desires can be factored into a simulation such as Nervana through factors already operating in the program. The detail of the desire algorithm, for example, will inevitably create small discontinuities that will result in apparently random desires.

The definitions given below give some indication of the initial framework for the philosophical background of the project. These definitions were superseded by those offered in Nervana Philosophic.

Subject - the subject in the Nervana Project is a simple humanoid ape. This does not mean that the subject in this theory cannot be as complex as a modern human. The idea being that if the Noble Ape in the Nervana Project has a^n complexity and the modern human has a^m complexity (where m>n) the Nervana Project will eventually reach very close to m. Chapter 8 covers this in greater detail.

Desire - the desires simulated in the Nervana Project remain within the simulation. They can be described though movements of the subjects and repeatable movements of single and multiple subjects, but as the simulation works, the desires cannot be translated to the real world. This parallels the real world=>human notion of desires. This is expanded upon in Chapters 6 and 7.

Past History - this is the intimate daily movements and interactions of the subject. These are described in the program as polymorphic constants which are manipulated and if found to be trivial or repetitive, 'forgotten' by the algorithm.

Desire Types (a possible mode of analysis?)

Natural Desire (needs)
(Food, Sleep, Safety, Reproduction,
Craving Desire (wants), Abstract Desire,
and Emotional Desire)

Are there any distinctions?

Natural desires (bar safety, which is an underlying desire-constant,) are governed by time. Food, or more importantly energy use is a micro-time dependent (second based) desire. Sleep is a mid-time dependent (minute based) desire and reproduction is a macro-time dependent (day based) desire. Natural desires are cumulative (i.e. if you do not eat or sleep for 24-hours, you will know you have not done this). These desires are not remembered, so a month after not eating or sleeping for 24-hours, one can still function without referring to this event.

Craving desires, I will argue, are time dependent as well. This may just be considered true through our society and the way people become creatures of habit. I fear that giving examples here would render me to criticism. The resolution for the time dependence of craving desires is taken in the early version of the Nervana Project to be hour based. The time dependent functions that need to be created in order for successful modeling will be discussed later.

The physics governing natural desires is discussed later in the manual, underlying natural desires is the need for survival. Many natural desires are connected with the other three desire types.

'I am hungry. I would like a sardine sandwich.'
Here a natural desire and a craving desire are connected.'

The simulation does not make any distinction between the different desire types as described briefly above. This analysis merely leads to the idea of a desire-access hierarchy that the user will come to empirically appreciate. Craving desires will be far more difficult for the user to access when compared to simple natural desires. The final application should allow for a user of the program to check on the energy remaining in each NA as well as whether or not they are tired and so on.

This framework was found to be erroneous, pretty early in the life of the project. However, it would appear to make the most sense of most of the manual presented and thus is one of the most quoted explanations of the project. Even though it is in fact not correct.

3. The Species

I have not studied biology formally since Year 10, so my knowledge of species interaction is purely empirical. I have purchased some books on biology and species. These include;

    Cambell, N A, 'Biology', Third Edition, Benjamin/Cummings Publishing, California, 1993
    Earl of Cranbrook, 'Mammals of South-East Asia', Second Edition, Oxford University Press, 1991
    Haas, P et al., 'Chemistry of Plant Products Vol I', Fourth Edition, Longmans, Green and Co., London, 1928
    Haas, P et al., 'Chemistry of Plant Products Vol II', Second Edition, Longmans, Green and Co., London, 1929

The simulation is set in an equatorial location and thus I have selected wildlife and vegetation very similar to regions of South-East Asia. This serves a romantic purpose, as well as a practical. I was enchanted in my four and a half months in South-East Asia by the diversity of wildlife and plant-life. It is questionable that such an island, as is simulated in Nervana, could exist in reality.

For simplification of calculation, there exists only two types of non-probability based creature, the NA and their foe, the Fierce Feline, every other type of creature has a wave probability of being found on the island. All creatures have a known population, so as species breed, die and are killed, real populations can be monitored.

    Animal Species
        Noble Ape
        Fierce Feline
        Herbivorous Mouse
        Insectivorous Mouse
        Sea-Bird
        Night-Bird
        Seed-Eating Bird
        Insectivorous Bird
        Ant
        Spider
        Fly
        Sea-Fish
    Plant Species
        Grass A

Grass B
Berry Bush
Bean Bush
Potato Plant
Fruit Bush
Flowering Bush A
Flowering Bush B
Berry Tree
Nut Tree
Non Descriptive Tree A
Non Descriptive Tree B
Non Descriptive Tree C
Boat Wood Tree

This section was initially plagued by tables that added nothing and made the whole section very difficult to read and understand if you printed the manual or viewed it in the wrong font. In order to remove this problem, I have divided each section into something more manageable and descriptive tables.

Herbivorous Diets

Ant
  Berry Tree
  Nut Tree
  Non Descriptive Tree A
  Non Descriptive Tree B
  Non Descriptive Tree C
  Boat Wood Tree

Seed Eating Bird
  Grass A
  Grass B
  Berry Bush
  Berry Tree
  Nut Tree

Herbivorous Mouse
  Grass B
  Berry Bush
  Bean Bush
  Potato Plant
  Fruit Bush
  Flowering Bush A
  Berry Tree

        Nut Tree

Noble Ape
        Berry Bush
        Bean Bush
        Potato Plant
        Fruit Bush
        Berry Tree
        Nut Tree

Carnivorous Diets

Noble Ape
        Fierce Feline
        Sea-Bird
        Sea-Fish
Fierce Feline
        Noble Ape
        Herbivorous Mouse
        Insectivorous Mouse
        Sea-Bird
        Night-Bird
        Seed-Eating Bird
        Insectivorous Bird
        Sea-Fish
Insectivorous Mouse
        Ant
        Spider
        Fly
Sea-Bird
        Sea-Fish
Night-Bird
        Herbivorous Mouse
        Insectivorous Mouse
        Sea-Fish
Insectivorous Bird
        Ant
        Spider
        Fly
Ant
        Ant
        Spider
        Fly

Spider
    Ant
    Spider
    Fly
Fly
    Any animal corpse
Sea-Fish
    ???

Description: Noble Ape

    Soon after announcing the BETA for this program, I started receiving emails from all over the world. Geologists and astronomers were worried that I had not included their disciplines in the description of the software. The geologists have now been consulted and added to this software, and version 1.01 will feature meteor showers. I am incorporating stargazing into the apes' hobby-list. Nevertheless, enough about this, apart from these people and VR-sters wanting to search for new algorithms for their own VR software, by far the most emails I received were concerning the apes. The apes quickly overtook the software as the star attraction, and it really would not matter if the software had been really poor, if the apes were funky then everyone would be happy. Hence the CD?

    The NA is a small human-like creature, commonly growing to only one and a half meters. They have a simple oral means of communication, although this notion is debated at great length in Chapters 7 and 8, and lead a nomadic life on the island. They tend not to be stocky and suffer the cold greatly. Winter is usually spent as a community group, sending out the stronger hunters and gatherers to collect food for the weaker members of the group. The spring is the season of renewal and the environment of the island changes greatly. The NAs break up into family groups and begin walking around the island. Summer tends to be spent near the ocean, as the mountain regions become too humid. The autumn time is spent building up food stocks for winter and finding a good camping spot for the group to congregate. The NA population that this software can support varies from 0 to 40. Later version of this software will support multiple islands and many more Noble Apes. The NA can live to about 30. Most die from illness in the winter months.

    The NA is generally a herbivore living off the nuts, legumes and berries that grow in the island's tree-covered region. Apart from this vegetation which is 'casually grazed upon', they will eat sea-fish and sea birds. The fierce feline is eaten on occasion. When one is killed, it is usually the time for great celebration on the island. The instances of a fierce feline killing a NA are far greater, and the apes are very cautious about approaching the island's cat population.

    I would imagine that the NAs' have an immense sense of being part of a larger scheme, and try not to abuse the environment. This is so much part of the NAs' philosophy, that in observing them one could attribute it to a pseudo-religious connection with the land. Trees that are cut to build fishing boats are always taken from different parts of the island. In a physical sense, this is a practical construct for energy restrictions.

Description: Fierce Feline

This is a medium to large sized cat, weighing 40-60kg. They live both in the trees and on the ground. The feline uses the trees as a look out for food as well as a means of ambushing its prey. They live for roughly 20 years, and can produce a litter of 4-6 kittens once a year after their first year. Real world creatures that are similar to these simulation creatures include the leopard cat and flat-headed cat of South East Asia.

Description: Herbivorous Mouse

This is the smallest of the two types of mice on the island. It is nocturnal and in the day returns to its burrow in the leaf litter of the jungle. In the real perspective of the project, these creatures should be a hybridization of a squirrel and a mouse. For this reason, they are slightly larger than their insectivorous cousins.

Description: Insectivorous Mouse

The insectivorous mice are nocturnal and more adventurous than their herbivorous cousins. They climb trees and explore the canopy branches in search of wayward insects.

Description: Sea-Bird

The sea-bird is a gull-like creature. It is almost entirely white.

Description: Night-Bird

The night-bird is modeled on the owls.

Description: Seed-Eating Bird

The seed eating bird is modeled on the parrots.

Description: Insectivorous Bird
Description: Ant
Description: Spider
Description: Fly
Description: Sea-Fish

There is an important message tucked away in Nervana and it is a message of conservation. All the creatures from the Nervana simulation are based on real living creatures that coexist through ever decreasing parts of South East Asia. Although national development in the region is a complex and sensitive issue, the wilderness in this region of the world supports millions of Nervana-like simulations.

Closer and more cosmetically an issue, the use of animals in 'medical' and 'scientific' tests raises real ethical questions when one believes that the animal operates with a similar means of information collection and processing. The propagation of primate ignorance through the educated world, as I see it, comes through fundamentalist Christian dogma that refuses to acknowledge the possibility of our Darwinian connection. With religious (and political) figures such as John-Paul II finally accepting the possibility of Darwinian evolution hopefully animal rights will improve. This is a vain hope when one examines the fact that most of the tests on animals are conducted by non-Creationist 'scientists'. This may just be a testament to the sterilization of modern science that again is exactly what the Nervana application tries to overcome.

4. The Mechanics

The history of the physics of the simulation could be elaborated in a set of manuals even larger than the existing texts. I have included the early arguments with a development into the ape vs. cat problem. The changes and developments of the mechanics of the simulation could be traced through;

>Newtonian mechanics, to,
>Heuristic approach, to,
>Lagrangian mechanics.

    Before I begin the historical account, I should give some explanation of these three approaches. Newtonian mechanics offer a series of equations that may be familiar through their filtering into popular culture. Force equals mass time acceleration. For every reaction, there is an equal and opposite reaction. The problem with this method is that it is not purposeful in a simulation. It can answer questions like, how much energy has been used by the apes in the past minute. Nevertheless, it does not act as a control method. There is nothing that stops a creature from accelerating or tells a creature to slow down because it is becoming tired. The Newtonian mechanical method requires a separate processing section to pose the questions of physics to it and then process the answers received.
    The heuristic approach says that non-physical equations that model reality are okay. These equations offer a close approximation and unlike the Newtonian mechanics method can be purposeful in that they can motivate changes in movement. This method appeared intoxicatingly simple. Until I realized the trap I had reached. I was no longer dealing with anything that could remotely be connected to real quantities; concepts of energy were replaced with concepts of tiredness and irritability. (Perhaps in a reflection of the author!) This method was a path to a false Nervana, because rather than creating answers to questions, I was creating questions with answers. The whole simulation could condense into a very simple heuristic game. If one treated the physics of the program heuristically, why not treat the program heuristically. It would begin with a beautiful start-up screen that would say, 'Welcome to Nervana. The program works!' and then it would quit. Because all the problems had been solved.
    Returning to the hard realities, from the realm of sarcasm, the heuristic approach led into the Lagrangian mechanics approach. The Lagrangian approach had one fundamental at its roots, energy is minimized. This simple point, via numerous equations became central to the simulation. As perhaps it should have initially. The minimization of energy in the physical realm solved all the possible physics problems, Nevertheless, like a pendulum it needed something to make it go. This came through the desire and fear structures in the simulation.

The text below represents the initial rigor of the physics that I wanted to implement. The response from David Pfitzner, comes after I sent him a discussion of how I wanted to implement the physic of the simulation with Newtonian mechanics and a time base of one minute.

The physics of the Nervana simulation is primarily used for the calculation of energy expenditure of the NAs on the island. After an elaborate set of debates that finished with the email below, I decided on a heuristic account of energy expenditure. The email remains for historical purposes and as an indication to the complexity of the calculation in terms of computer time per NA, per minute, and also the fact that the final result is long winded and has serious frictional error problems.

From: David Pfitzner
To: Tom Barbalet
Subject: Principia Physica Nervana

...

Following is a first-pass at how _I_ think Nervana motion physics should work, if it's to be based on real physics. ("If it were done, t'were best it were done... reasonably....")

Assume we have a surface $(x,y,fz(x,y))$, and consider the motion of a single NA (Nervana Automata :-) on this surface. As well as the height of the surface, we will need the vector normal to the surface at each point (i.e. to give information about the `slope' of the surface). (I.e. the normal is the direction perpendicular to that plane which is a tangent to the surface at this point :-)

If the normal vector is (nx, ny, nz), with magnitude 1, and $nz>0$ everywhere, then given local slopes dz/dx and dz/dy, one has

$nz = 1/sqrt(1 + (dz/dx)^2 + (dz/dy)^2)$
$nx = -nz\ dz/dx$
$ny = -nz\ dz/dy$

(i.e. given tabulated $fz(x,y)$, can calc n vector at each point using finite differences to calc dz/dx and dz/dy.) (Derivation: trig gives the second two, and then magnitude=1 gives the first.)

At a given time the NA has a position (x,y) (=> z), and, say, a velocity, (vx, vy, vz). We will require that the NA stays on the surface, so that the velocity must remain _in_ the surface; i.e. be perpendicular to the normal. This means that given (vx, vy), can obtain

$vz = (-1/nz)\ (vx\ nx + vy\ ny)$

At the next time step, after time dt, the new positions (indicated by primed quantities) are approximated by

$x' = x + vx\ dt$
$y' = y + vy\ dt$
and z' is simply $z' = fz(x',y')$.

(I.e. actually you didn't need to calculate vz to get z', be wait...)

How to get the corresponding new velocities? For an energy-conservative system, conservation of energy gives some constraints, but in general doesn't specify everything (e.g. direction of the velocity). Consider instead forces. The NA always experiences a gravitational force,

$Fgrav* = - m\ g\ z*$

Where '*' indicates a vector quantity, and $z*$ is the unit vector in the z direction (a totally non-standard notation I just made up now). The NA also experiences a force from the surface. E.g., when the NA is stationary on a flat surface, then this surface force exactly balances the gravitational force, so there is no net force, and so no change in motion. When the situation is less simple, I'm going to claim that the surface force is always in the direction of the normal vector.
(I can't give a good reason at the moment, but I think this is correct...)
I.e.

$Fsurf* = Fsurf\ n*$

(where Fsurf is the magnitude, and Fsurf* the 3-component vector).
The magnitude Fsurf must be such that the velocity at the new time is again within the surface (at the new position (x',y')). The force is

$Ftot*\quad = Fgrav* + Fsurf*$
$\quad\quad\quad = Fsurf\ nx\ x* + Fsurf\ ny\ y* + (Fsurf\ nz - m\ g)\ z*$

The new velocities are

$vx' = vx + ax\ dt = vx + (Fx/m)\ dt$

etc, i.e.

$vx' = vx + (Fsurf/m)\ nx\ dt$
$vy' = vy + (Fsurf/m)\ ny\ dt$
$vz' = vz + (Fsurf/m)\ nz\ dt - g\ dt$

Now use

$vz = (-1/nz)\ (\ vx\ nx + vy\ ny\ )$

and also

$vz' = (-1/nz') (vx' nx' + vy' ny')$

and solve for Fsurf in terms of $(nx,ny,nz), (nx',ny',nz'), (vx,vy,vz), m, g$, since these are all know quantities. I.e.

$vz + (Fsurf/m) nz\, dt - g\, dt = (-1/nz') (vx' nx' + vy' ny')$
=>
$(-1/nz)(vx\, nx + vy\, ny) + (Fsurf/m) nz\, dt - g\, dt = (-1/nz')(vx\, nx' + (Fsurf/m) nx\, nx'\, dt + vy\, vy' + (Fsurf/m) ny\, ny'\, dt)$
=>
$(Fsurf/m)\, dt\, (nz + nx\, nx'/nz' + ny\, ny'/nz') = g\, dt + vx\, nx/nz + vy\, ny/nz - vx\, nx'/nz' - vy\, ny'/nz'$
=>
$(Fsurf/m)\, dt = (g\, dt + vx\, nx/nz + vy\, ny/nz - vx\, nx'/nz' - vy\, ny'/nz') / (nz + nx\, nx'/nz' + ny\, ny'/nz')$

I.e. feed this value into above equations to get (vx', vy'), and the NA has been advanced one time step.

(Exercise: is the result energy conserving for small enough time-steps?)

Advantage of is approach is that can add other forces, e.g.:

- friction:
    static: (when $vx=vy=0$) force opposed to ($Fsurf^* + Fgrav^*$), up to maximum constant value to give $Ftot^*=0$
    dynamic: force whose value depends on velocity (proportional to v^2?), with direction opposite to velocity.- self motion: i.e. force due to the NA, to move according to desires etc. probably in any direction perpendicular to normal. implies internal energy being expended by NA.

Problems/issues:
- details of these extra forces... :-)
- how do these forces affect the derivation of Fsurf above? (before/after?)
- how to implement the internal-energy cost of the self-motion force? (i.e. I think the simple $dE = F\, ds$, while probably on the right track, and maybe applicable in restricted circumstances, is _not_ the full story.)
- for numerical integration it's usually more accurate (and stable etc) to have a leapfrog method, where positions and velocities are updated at alternate half-time-steps respectively, for somewhat increased complication...

Actually, the calculation of Fsurf probably mucks this up anyway...

The first feature I should probably explain about the Nervana simulation is the units used in the description of mass and energy are slightly different to SI units as used in physics. Food is consumed over time and as it is consumed, it releases energy into the body at a delayed rate. The physics of food/energy release, much like the physics of sleep and need for sleep, could be the topic of vast treatise in themselves. The table below gives a rough indication of the time taken to consume food and the energy gained from each kind of food. Obviously, the time taken to absorb the food is related to the hunger of the eater and some movement factors. For example, a starving cat finally catching and consuming its prey will not die due to hunger in the interim of digestion.

Food	Energy for NA	Energy for FF
Fruit from bushes [B]	200±80/min	-
Sea-Fish [S]	300±100/min(5-20 min)	3000±1000/min(1-2 min)
Mice [M]	-	300±100(1 min)
Sea-Bird [E]	90±30/min(4-10 min)	900±300(1 min)
Night-Bird [N]	-	1200±400(1 min)
Seed-Eating Bird [D]	-	300±100(1 min)
Insectivorous Bird [V]	-	450±150(1 min)
Fierce Feline	600±200/min(20-40 min)	-
Noble Ape	-	6000±2000/min(3-5 min)

I do not allow the energy to enter the system of the creature instantly. To avoid logarithmic energy digestion equations that take mathematics and biology too far, as far as I am concerned, I will talk about the food transfer following this equation;

$$de = a / 20$$

Where a is the initial amount of energy. This is taken when the creature stops eating, and the de is measured in minutes as per the simulation. If a creature stops eating for a minute then this equation is fired and sends the de into their system. The maximum energy a creature can consume is based on their size. This factor varies from 2 to 200 in NA and 1 to 60 in FF. Because the NA and FF digestive systems are different, they have different energy storage equations.

There are some energy totals that are crucial to understand.

Maximum stored energy (stomach max)
Actual stored energy (stomach now)   S
Maximum metabolized energy (system max)

Actual metabolized energy (system now)   M
Rate of energy used   dE

M = de - dE

When de is fired, it must be substantially larger than dE.

From, $dE = 1/2\, m\, v^2$, it is best that we simply work from the mass and velocity to the dE. This is just a simple method of attributing a real physical link. This energy equation is too idealized for these purposes. $dE = m\, v^2$ offers the right dimensions and allows for some composite friction. The units are not important anyway.

Most NAs velocities would be 0 to 200 units/minute (max ~400) (a unit being 0.25m) (0 - 3km/hr max 6km/hr), most FF velocities would be 0 to 2000 units/minute (max ~3000) (0 - 30km/hr max 45km/hr).

Let us introduce another Dungeons and Dragons concept that I will call maximum velocity.

v(NA) = 2s
v(FF) = 50s

Where s is the size of the creature. Now the NA spread of maximum speed is linear.

p = v(NA) - v

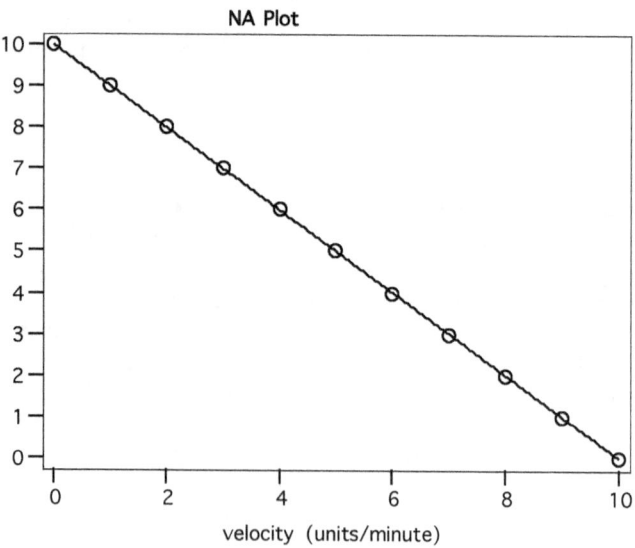

Where p is the average that must really be divided by the integral of p for a percentage of that speed on the graph. The FF has a parabolic graph for speed.

p = v(FF)^2 - v^2

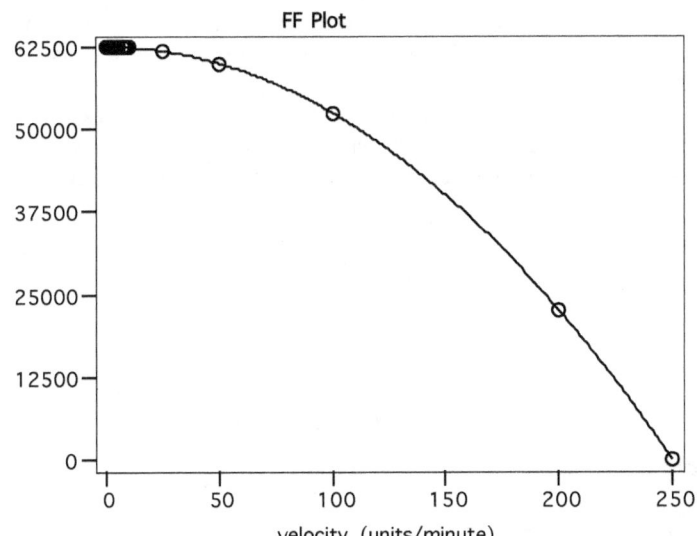

Both graphs are for a creature of size 5 (very small). One can see that the p value is useless and p needs to be calculated relative to the area under the curve.

NA

p = v(NA) - v
∂ = kv - 1/2 v^2 = v(NA)^2 / 2

FF

p = v(FF)^2 - v^2
∂ = k^2v - 1/3 v^3 = 2 v(FF) ^3 / 3
b = p/∂

The motivation for movement at lower speeds comes through the energy expenditure. Thus, a creature will only move at high speeds when they have to. This should be understood as a secondary effect of the simulation there is no control of the creature's speed through an argument along the lines of;

Animal A has been moving for too long at speed B. They must slow down!

The difference between forced movement and formula persuaded movement is an abstract argument that may prove difficult to understand. If we try to imagine a small child when they have just learnt to walk - they may want to try out this new mode of transport for as long as possible. Yet eventually they will get tired and collapse. Over time, they will realize that walking is best done for controlled periods of time, but nothing external affects them! The only thing that affects them is there expenditure of energy.

Large parts of the Nervana simulation 'work' for these reasons. Not because the program constructs an 'if...then...' clause, but through the fact that something happens based on some algebraic construction which limits the final outcome.

The most important mechanics that exists in the simulation is the way that species survive, particularly species in the middle or bottom of the food chain.

The physics of the food chain became intertwined with the linear algebra analysis of population densities. Two topics that must rate a mention are the division of time and the point calculation for the apes and the cats.

The division of time has been a real problem in the simulation. While writing it on a 16Mhz 68000, I chose the minute to be the basis of time. Moving up to a PowerPC processor, the minute just became that much faster. My experience of the G3, while working on Escape From Nervana showed me a processor that would not only eat through any virtual reality interface I could write but also a processor which could run second steps rather than minute steps.

With the development of Iota 0.5, which had at its heart the same infinite virtual reality creation engine as Escape From Nervana, I began to ponder the quantization issues of the simulation. The old Nervana and Iota simulation had quantized land to 25m! The new Escape From Nervana engine had taken that down to 72cm at a pinch. For a space that was 3.2km by 3.2km, that was quite a bit of detail. Nevertheless, it could easily be taken to roughly 20cm, or even about 5cm. Such a small resolution for such a large area challenged the possibility that the time resolution could be reduced as well. This was initially the biggest barrier to realism. It should be noticed that the visualization algorithm as tested on the PowerPC had still been slightly less than real time. This was a fundamental slow point that needed an evil heuristic approximation to be made.

The point calculation for the apes and the cats was another problem. Therefore, central to the simulation was the problem that it was written up in the document, 'Cat/Ape Problem'. This problem was simple. An island inhabited with points. Some of the points have the properties exhibited by apes. Some of the points have properties exhibited by cats. The fundamental outcome for both species was survival, and survival around the other species. The simulation up until this point had treated the creatures within it as population densities. All the 'lower' creatures on the island together with the plants and animals were mapped with wave functions over the island. The solution to these wave functions gave some indication of the survival rate of these creatures. Nevertheless, the apes and the cats were different. They existed as moving points in the simulation, and in the game Escape From Nervana. Much of the development of the ape vs. cat problem was motivated by the development of Escape From Nervana. The apes needed to have method of survival that did not require the human user to play each ape at the same time. This problem is not a simple matter of solving a couple of equations and then writing a game around it. The analysis offered in the companion text, gives some indication of the possible methods of approach of any of the physical problems encountered through the simulation.

5. The Program

The exoskeleton of the program was designed to be as fast and as minimalist as possible. The main arrays in the application are;

> the sine dump
> land height in the x-axis, land height in the y-axis, dz/dx x-axis, dz/dy y-axis
> NAs' location, direction-facing, age, condition etc.

The remainder of the application is taken by local variables except for macro state variables and the time, date and weather information.

All the mathematics in the application is integer based. The use of sine and co-sine variables comes from points over 2-pi sine dump with a fixed large resolution. Initially the number chosen was 840 because of its factorial properties, but later it was changed to 1024, for its binary properties! Technically, it could be even larger, but it does fit some good credentials at the present size.

Just as an aside, I have always been interested in relatively small numbers with a high number of factorials. The largest long integer (32-bits) I have found with the highest number of factorials is 232792560 with 960 factorials. The largest integer (15 or 16-bits) is 27720 with 96 factorials.

The Nervana file handling system is almost exclusively text based. This allows the user to access and alter certain parameters in the program if they see fit. Most Nervana variables are 4-bit hexadecimal numbers. Unusually, these are represented in Nervana with the letters A to P (or sometimes Q). The highest order 4-bits will always be written first.

A	-8	0
B	-7	1
C	-6	2
D	-5	3
E	-4	4
F	-3	5
G	-2	6
H	-1	7
I	0	8
J	1	9
K	2	10
L	3	11
M	4	12
N	5	13
O	6	14

```
P    7   15
Q    8
```

The Nervana genetic-land description is shown in a file as;

<NerG>ABCDEFGHIJ

It is important that this information is contained in the beginning of the text file as it describes the layout of the island. The '<NerG>' section is called the description. That tells the program firstly that it is a legitimate Nervana genetic land description. The remaining section represents the ten parameters from -8 to 8 (A to Q) as described in LAND. To refresh the memory here is the formula for land creation;

$f(x) = sd[x] + sd[2*x]\backslash(4*gen[1]) + sd[3*x]\backslash(4*gen[2]) + sd[4*x]\backslash(4*gen[3]) + sd[5*x]\backslash(4*gen[4]) + sd[6*x]\backslash(4*gen[5])$

$g(y) = sd[y] + sd[2*y]\backslash(4*gen[6]) + sd[3*y]\backslash(4*gen[7]) + sd[4*y]\backslash(4*gen[8]) + sd[5*y]\backslash(4*gen[9]) + sd[6*y]\backslash(4*gen[10])$

The gen numbers correspond to the following in <NerG>ABCDEFGHIJ;

```
1     A
2     C
3     E
4     G
5     I
6     B
7     D
8     F
9     H
10    J
```

An easy way to imagine it is through thinking;

<NerG>xyxyxyxyxy

With the xs and the ys following the more and more wavy lines down the line.

The next information that a Nervana file should contain is information about the NA locations on the island. This is represented by a single method in this version, but I for-see future versions having many more advanced methods of NA description.

```
<NerA>
    AA
    AAA,   AAA,   A
    ^      ^     ^
    x      y     facing
```

For historical reasons I have kept this colorful aside about the formation of inland water ways. It gives some indication of a time in the project where I became overly obsessed with realism.

Now we have covered so much of the island and the species construction in the Nervana simulation I shall add the concept of inland water as a possibility. This comes in two flavors, lakes and streams. Lakes are defined as the filling of local minima on the planer map of the island (i.e. cups in the land) and streams are defined as the shortest route down from the lakes.

The mathematically astute (those who are still reading) will recognize that the bottom of a lake can be found with many methods. The one I will chose to use is a fast programming technique. However, before I bamboozle with sign logic, let us examine what the maximum number of lakes on an island can be. I will argue that four is the maximum number that can exist. My argument goes like this; a sine wave produces lows and highs (corresponding with -1 and 1 respectively).

1	high						
2	high	low					
3	high	low	high				
4	high	low	high	low			
5	high	low	high	low	high		
6	high	low	high	low	high	low

The only lows that interest us in the formation of lakes are the lows with highs on either side as these produce the safe saddle dip which you need for a lake.

3	high	low	high			
5	high	low	high	low	high

Now if this is cumulatively added the best result which can be gained for lake formation is;

    high   low   high   low   high

Nevertheless, this represents one dimension of the two dimensional land surface. Two lows times two lows gives four lake possibilities. Of course these lakes may not exist, do not assume anything! However, if they do, we will have allocated memory for the x and y coordinates for them. Now to find them take f(x) or g(x) and progress across using the rule that;

$$x1 = f(x-1)$$
$$x2 = f(x)$$
$$x3 = f(x+1)$$

There exists a minima where;

$$x2 < x1 \leq x3$$

This should be taken at the maximum resolution of the graph, particularly when the possibility of $x1=x2$ or even worse $x1=x2=x3$ is quite probably with any rounded division of f(x).

Carry out this process in the g(y) plane and there may exist up to four minima points stored in px1, px2, py1, py2 (for 'possible x point number 1'...etc). The possibilities we shall consider are;

    no minima
    one minima
    two minima
    more than two minima

For the no or one case, no lake can exist. For the two case, a lake can only exist if one is from f(x) and one is from g(y) and for the more than two case, there are at least two lakes.

Having completed this there may exist up to four lakes with defined minima. Now we must find the associated maxima with each giving a high on either side of the low. This is done again in the separate dimensions for speed and points max1 and max2 are found on either side of px. There must exist such points for the definition of the minima to hold. Now whichever of the two maxima points is less (in f(x)) is defined as the run off point if both are equal this is important.

Now taking both dimensions, there may exist a point (x,y) with two maxima in the f(x) plane and two in the g(y) plane. If the maxima for f(x) are equal and the maxima for g(y) are equal then there are no rivers from this lake (folks). However, if one dimension is equal and the other is not then, there will exist two rivers and if both dimensions have single specific run off point then there will be one river. Rivers follow down the steepest possible route that is nearly always towards the sea and obviously this route remains constant. Thus, a file with the rivers format in it should contain the following information

number of minima for f(x)
number of minima for g(y)
location x1, x2, y1, y2 (if existent)
location of the corresponding run off points (only, not all maxima needed)

Having created this definition, surely I have created a problem for all the future uses of the water operator and also graphing. The water collected in the lakes and rivers is fresh. This other operator needs to be created - but this operator will just obey the existing water operator and the fish that are found in these water-ways have the same stats as the already existing sea-fish.

This system dramatically slows mapping and the Vector 3 graphing algorithm as the new fresh water systems have to be mapped dynamically around the flow point.

I used to write an anti-viral program with a simple command line interface, intertwined into the GUI. I have always believed that an intelligent (or at least not very stupid) command line interface can open the application up for mass information acquisition. There is a modern fear of command line interfaces, particularly through MS-DOS and long UNIX commands. Before one starts in fear at the thought of learning a whole series of useless commands, I will explain two things. Nevertheless, before I will begin, the Nervana command-line interface is called NCI (for Nervana Command-line Interface).

No commands over three characters
Intelligent command recognition

All the NCI commands can be used with three characters or even less through the intelligent command recognition interface.

The important commands that I have thought of are;

view
all stats, all apes
specific stats, all apes
all stats, specific ape
specific stats, specific ape
all stats, all cats
specific stats, all cats
all stats, specific cat
specific stats, specific cat
all populations
specific populations

stats

age
location x,y,f
sex
size
id number
current speed
d energy
energy stored
energy consumed
father id
mother id
status (this includes things like injured, pregnant for x days etc)

goto time in the future
date and time
name
ape
feline

The simulation in the future will allow for 4294967296 apes to be created (32-bit id number). A user can register (for free) as many apes as they wish (before they are 'born') and will be given a computer id number from which every ape they create will be uniquely stamped. This process should yield a vast population of uniquely created apes with their own identities from millions of different islands. Feline records will also be considered, although no long term information is stored on the cats.

6. Sex, Birth, Life and Death - Existence Through Emotion

When one looks at these five, one can create some kind of causation argument.

> From birth comes life.
> From life comes birth.
> From life comes death.

One can be too clinical about this analysis, but the primary purpose of the program is to simulate life. Death and birth comes through certain conditions being filled in the program and birth comes at a time after sex. Let me offer and argument about how the ape's sex affects the ape. Male dominance is not written into the program - and moreover it is a system that is not universal to all societies of creatures on the planet. I would argue that a sex's dominance is a secondary effect of the location of the simulation. Different islands offer different situations. The only difference between the male and female NAs in any practical sense is that they are distinguishable and the males grow slightly larger - up unto the point of reproduction.

Now what governs two apes getting together for a little quality time? There are many possible answers. Firstly, one must ask questions of population, social groups, what kind of society do the creatures exist in? These are too complicated for questions that the application can answer and moreover the application does not pose questions to the creatures on the island 'Hello, Ape #8342, are you feeling hungry currently?'. Reproduction is a condition that is (ahem) satisfied when a male and female ape coexist on the same point in the simulation, under certain condition, but there are a number of reasons that this can occur. Almost all exclusively hormonal or more importantly temporal.

The next section of text has been included in these documents, because many readers of the manual have said to me that it is the ONLY section of the manual they remember with clarity. I have included it for the benefit of those who have requested it.

However, just for fun I with play a thought experiment with you. This is a philosophical question that has haunted me since childhood, and a question that one nearly got me thrown out of mathematics tutorial at University. The question is simple, 'Do rabbits fall in love?'

If you answer no, your argument can be based on rabbit populations and the speed at which rabbits multiply. Surely, this would only be possible if they were promiscuous. I have never read any study of rabbit sexual ethics, and although there exists a lot of text on primate sexuality and a lot of material on other creatures down the food chain, I have never read anything about rabbit's sexual choices. The primary argument for people saying no is simple, if they feel anything it is purely lust.

To play the devil's advocate, I will always argue that rabbits do fall in love. It is an interesting argument piece actually, because many people will argue their side so passionately - and hence my near eviction from the math tutorial. I argue that rabbits do fall in love because they have such short term memories that there must be something more than simple lust going on in their heads. My test-group of rabbits come through my brothers' pet rabbits, starting off with a rabbit called Thumper. The test rabbits names are Thumper, Fluffy and Hazel (from Hazelra of Watership Down). Thumper was the first rabbit my brother Felix owned. My other brother David owned a rabbit called Loco, but he quickly died of cancer. Thumper, however, was house trained very quickly and developed a taste for mouthwash. Mouthwash had high alcohol content and turned the rabbit totally pawless. Thumper was a miserable alcoholic, but very placid and always welcome to some bizarre psychological experiments. May I point out that Thumper was never harmed and only growled when he had a hangover. Felix derived an experiment to find out how long Thumper's memory lasted by putting him in the corner of a room and seeing how long it took him to turn around. With no alcohol in his system, the rabbit would quickly hop around and hop towards the closest person, but even after a little mouthwash Thumper would remain in the corner, just staring at the wall. Felix argued that this was because his memory existed for such short bits of time that he could not remember how he had gotten there.

FLASH!

This is new, I am staring at the wall.

FLASH!

This is new, I am staring at the wall.

FLASH!

This is new, I am staring at the wall.

FLASH!

This is new, I am staring at the wall.

I always suspected Thumper sustained extensive brain damage from alcohol abuse. Thumper was always solitary apart from the occasional affair with neatly folded pajamas, but he could never get the pajamas drunk enough to get what he wanted, he was always too drunk himself, or he was busted by a concerned brother or mother.

Thumper was a Canberra rabbit, but in Kuala Lumpur, Malaysia, my brothers kept two rabbits called Fluffy and Hazel - who were very much lovers and had many litters to prove it. There were little things that made me think that these two had something special. Primarily the fact they would lie pushing their snouts outside the wire towards one another as they slept. (The of course lived in separate cages - although jail breaks produced litters.) My argument of rabbit love is not conclusive in any sense, but one must still wonder what brings rabbits together. Does one rabbit stare at the other and think, 'My, those are a nice set of teeth', 'What big ears!' or perhaps, 'What a beautiful white tail he has'?

Moreover, just when you think I have spent too many late nights studying my virtual apes, I will return to the original topic. What makes one ape become attracted to another ape? Like the real estate agents say, 'Location! Location! Location!' The apes need to be close to be close! I would argue this is just a practical constraint due to lack of postal service or telephone or internet connection for that matter. There are no long distance relationships on the island. Therefore, the NA need to be in the same region and moreover need to know each other through sight. Rape does occur on the island. This is very difficult to write into a simulation of this sort, but it fits into the psychological desire structure that I will begin to explain a little later in this chapter. Let us rule out rape for the moment in terms of the NA romance. Let us ask an abstract question, are NA libel to form life-long relationships? Like the five year old, I would have to answer, 'Depends...' It really depends on the island and the social mean. If the society is designed for life-long relationships, through Bo's argument of a mean ape, then this is the social pattern.

Before I go any further, I should acknowledge that many of these frustrating circular questions will be answered in the next chapter with an analysis of identity through vision. The best way to offer answers to the questions that I am posing is through a question of what is internal and what external information is. What is an internal emotion and what is an external interaction with the outside world?

Now this may seem like another stupid circular question, but this is not my intention. As a somewhat difficult initial example, let us try to tackle the concept of love. We shall rely on the fact that emotions are meta-reasonable things. That is, if we think about why we feel the way we do we can usually come up with some reasonable outcome. This is not an existential claim. I am not saying that there exists good reason for every emotion - but there exists a real set of information which may be generated over a long period of time which can explain every reaction. The question that I pose later is 'Can this logical progression of information that we construct after actions to explain actions, be actively used in a simulation sense or does this notion go against causality and determination?'

I think it is foolish to get into an argument that goes something along the lines of;

'We humans are far too complicated to comprehend what makes us tick!'

This is not only defeatist but it is also elitist and it is a mode of thought that will not yield any solution to any problem. The way one should think when one is writing or using a simulation is that everything that we cover with some degree of mysticism is in fact something that should be relatively straight forward with the correct analytical method. This is fundamental to polymorphic analysis, and is one of the most controversial, but also rewarding aspects of polymorphic thought. If a system appears complex or impossible to solve it is purely because the right method has not been thought of yet - and not because the solution is impossible. Just for the record, this is fundamental to polymorphic theory and I find it a liberating notion that enables much expanded thought.

I begin this argument to identify a mode of thought that I think is erroneous but runs rife in modern philosophy and that is of convoluted ideas used as fundamentals. Now many would argue that I may be guilty of exactly this sin when I construct a Water operator with a Height operator i.e. that the water level is dependent on the Height and thus any construction of water in fact comes directly from Height. Nevertheless, I will put this criticism down for the moment - and return to it for the full judgment it deserves later in this section. Be wary as well, as I am leading down a long road towards the question of love.

I wish to develop a theory that I will call Numerical Epistemology or NE (just to become confused with NA). I shall begin by describing epistemology as I think it is an interesting topic and one that has been exploited by many areas that are genuinely ignorant of the true scope of the study. Epistemology is the Philosophy of Knowledge or the Study of Knowledge as it may be described internally by philosophers. If I may digress a little, I will explain why I chose not to overuse the term epistemology. This comes from the introduction I received to epistemology in a series of lectures on Plato - in my first year of university. We had a very aerobic lecturer who performed this lecturer on epistemology in front of a blackboard with a giant penis drawn on it - which he did not notice over the lecture. Throughout the lecture, the fellow avoided turning and using the board on a number of occasions. It was almost impossible to sit in the lecture and either listen or look directly at this man waving his hands in front of this drawing of the genitals that was as tall as he was. Double this by the school-boys toilet humor value of the term he was lecturing about and I fear that the piss was forever taken out of the word epistemology. Now I am over that digression, I will start with my numerical arguments.

This chapter is forever intertwined with the concepts that I create in the next chapter and I am writing both sections parallel avoiding the use of any mathematics in this chapter and just developing rigorous verbal explanations of what I do with math in the next chapter. This is done first, so I introduce quite complicated concepts with the first numerical equations in the next chapter.

The Philosophy of Knowledge is really complex series of twists and turns which covers most of philosophical thought including concepts such as Aesthetics.

Aesthetics in popular terms means the appreciation and understanding of beauty, the Philosophy of Art or my preferred definition, the science of sense-perception. This development from sensory information into some kind of existential truth is what the next two chapters are really about. An expansion of visual information is offered in the next chapter - the important point in this chapter is what exists inside. What is really a motivating factor in our existence and what generates the desires that motivate movement and interaction with the outside world? The love of a rabbit for example. A fundamental reason we move is to collect food and this should not be under estimated in any way, shape or form. These structures that motivate our motions such as earning money so we can purchase food and shelter are social constructs which the NA would not have to deal with in the initial realms of the simulation. I am not trying to be defeatist in any way by offering this analysis - merely trying to offer the scope of analysis that is purely Nervana related initially.

What simplification or reduction of desires needs to be conducted which does not lose any of the information in the process? This is where I began with the concept of convoluted ideas being used as fundamentals. We need to construct some fundamental idea of what makes an emotion or a desire. I will offer an analysis that is similar to the one applied to in Appendix C. Let us take an abstract example that I use often when describing the simulation. A young ape sees a member of their family, say their mother, killed by a feline. This is the only example the child has of the feline as a creature. This ape develops a fear of the feline that results in a number of other fear-features such as a fear of the dark jungle for example.

The next chapter develops a rigorous argument that describes both what static and moving objects are to the observing creature in the simulation. Let us assume that this is already given and the observing NA child can understand both what the feline is as a unique creature and what all felines are - in an abstract sense. Now how does the child form a connection with fear? Moreover, what is fear? I can produce a rigorous argument that says that fear is the only productive emotion and thus the only emotion that we should be interested in a simulation sense, but this quite a boring proof and one that I feel goes against intuition. Nevertheless, for the simple analysis I will offer the mono emotional argument.

Mono emotional argument

There exists an emotional operator that is applied to objects or the absence of objects in order to produce movement. This emotional operator is the fear operator.

`F   It describes a condition where the creature has a desire to leave the current position.

Please note the` represents an emotional operator not to be confused with the island operators. Although I promised no mathematics I have to offer some symbols that represent time, movement (or in physics terms velocity), objects and identity.

space	s
time	t
movement	v (comes through traveling through space in time)
objects	o (comes from perception of space through movement)
identity	i (which comes from the other four points)

It is important to understand that all of the above are very different and inhabit different realms of time for want of a better word. We as living human creatures experience the world from instant to instant. This in physics is called dt and it enables us to see movement that is called velocity in physics and has the description ds/dt.

Now what has all this got to do with emotions, life, death and sex? Why am I talking about physics? Because physics is essentially the description of the real world with numbers and a means of developing theories about the real world with numbers (hence the Numerical Epistemology name). In addition, I wish to describe emotions and desires with numbers as well. Please note that I say numbers and not true or false statements. This is roughly covered in the Frequently Asked Questions document sent out with the simulation, but if you missed reading it, I will include the section concerning Rules (which develop true and false answers) and Laws (which develop infinite possibilities of answers).

1. What are the differences between Nervana and the Sim series from Maxis?

The primary difference is that Nervana is free and the Sim series are all commercial pieces of software. There is no real comparison between Nervana and the Sim series in terms of simulation principles. The Sim series use trick algorithms that con the user into believing that the program is really simulating something. The rules for Sim City for example were so simple that the game quickly became boring no matter what land formation was found, if you knew the rules for residential building etc. There are no such rules in the Nervana simulation, because the Nervana application is not governed by rules, but by laws. The simple difference is that rules force if...then... situations, where as laws are more 'linear' and offer infinite solutions. Laws also are used sparingly and minimally - the ideal is to have a simulation that only has a few simple laws (energy, sickness etc) and has a whole series of secondary effects coming from those laws. Nothing controls the speed at which a creature moves in the simulation for example except the restraining force of loss of energy. Therefore, although a large cat can move at great speed, they will not over a long period of time because they become exhausted.

2. What is the difference between rule-based life simulations and infinite virtual reality simulations?

There are many fundamental differences between rule-based life simulations and infinite virtual reality simulations. The latter is far more stable an environment for simulation and offers an extremely high resolution if needed. The Nervana simulation's infinite virtual reality engine could easily simulate to a resolution of a centimeter of even smaller with only simple modifications of the existing code. There are no rules in the Nervana Simulation, everything fits together with simple laws that should not be confused with rules. The key differences are;

	Laws	Rules
Number of choices at any point	∞	2
Resolution	almost infinitesimal	coarse
Reaction to unpredicted data	good	unable to handle
Occam's razor applicable?	yes	unable to handle
Used in description of the real world	yes	no*
Code implementation	small	large
Compactness	yes	no
Uniqueness	yes	unable to handle
Layered development and modification	yes	very difficult
force law	$F=ma$	if there is a mass and there is acceleration then there is a force

* perhaps through argument in legal circles, but even then not absolute

Now I have offered some form of description of how and why I am going to formulate NE, let us return to the description of the complex emotional reaction to identify the fundamental points. (Please note that a more detailed and personal account is given of this process in Chapter 8 - concerning the possibility and the depth than one can practically do this in the Nervana simulation.

- A young ape sees a member of their family, say their mother, killed by a feline.

The observer is the young ape, obviously. Concepts that the young ape needs to understand include:

Mother
Killed
Feline

With the fear analysis, the mother is the negation of fear. We should understand that fear is a numerical value that is constructed through a collection of objects that the observer can see. The concept of object, see and observer are all defined in the next chapter. Now although the observer can see the objects 'Mother' and 'Feline', it can also so a whole series of other things. The observer knows the location where they are in their own 'mind' (i.e. they have a mental location). This can come from specific objects they can see - the shape of the land for example, various dead trees etc. Also objects that are very abstract like darkness, shadows or the inability to see the horizon.

As a digression, the inability to see the horizon is an important piece of information. Just as the inability to what is coming up can also induce fear. From this analysis one can see that sequential objects - that is object that follow one from another - are very important. Nevertheless, have I led you into a thought trap? (Perhaps might I add a little accidentally.)

An ability to see the horizon induces fear in the NA - which is where their fundamental fear of water comes from. Therefore, a situation where the NA's vision is surrounded and they cannot see the horizon should offer some degree of security. This is something like the Malaysian country taxi drivers who only overtake when they can see the other car coming in the opposite direction. Not that I am linking country Malaysian taxi drivers with the NA - but I think there is something remarkably intuitive about this approach to existence and it makes my theory of vision somewhat more connected. Now where does the fear of the horizon come from? I would argue that it comes from concepts of infinity that the NA cannot process. In fact, distance as created in the next chapter, is totally described by personal experience and motion through space - the NA could not move through enough space in order to have a physical understanding of how far the horizon is. Moreover, the NA are very short sighted. They have a maximum range of vision of roughly 800m - which is nowhere near our understanding of the horizon (roughly 14km).

Nevertheless, what does fear mean? In addition, what is all this business about operators and things?

To put it simply an operator is a piece of mathematics that you bung before or sandwich between other bits of mathematics to get a different result. In the case of the fear operator, it is applied to the creature's collection of fear variables and produces a reaction instantly - in the form of movement.

The ape is walking along, sees a big cat come and eat his mother and fear kicks in instantly. This is the difference between fear and so many other emotions, is although it can creep up on the fearful and have some increasing properties - it happens considerably faster than the desire that you have just woken and feel hungry.

This may appear to be a bit of a hand waving exercise to try to arrange a simple view of the world - with a little math thrown in to add to the mysticism - but there really is a practical argument tucked up inside this idea. The idea being that instantaneous chemical reactions - adrenaline etc - being sent into the brain is considerably more fundamental and fast than abstract concepts like, 'I want that cute ape over there, thank you very much, yes sireee...'

Nevertheless, what does this mono-emotional analysis offer us? A very confused world view indeed, many may argue. One needs to try to construct arguments that create all possible emotional reactions through fear alone.

love - the fear of being alone
anger - constricted fear
happiness - absence of fear

Nevertheless, how does one describe lust or even love, anger and happiness sensibly within a simulation? Enter (after a substantial drum role and much thought) the desire operator.

Fear and Desire

The desire operator is considerably more complicated than just simple fear. Whereas fear is a fast reaction relating to objects (which can also include places - as places are just landscape objects), desire as defined here is a process that can justify movement. This description offers little insight into the true depth of desire and it is important to note early into my account of NE, that the word 'desire' now should leave the popular meaning of the term and apply to the following definition.

The desire operator takes the information stored in the creatures identity - that is not only the information of space mapped on time, but also the collection of objects generated and their particular fear characteristics - and develops a movement over time that is not based in the velocity of escape (as the fear operator is) but is based in the gaining of reaching an object (which as previously defined also includes places).

What this says is that desire is not about escaping at speed, like fear, but it is concerned with the reaching of a place where the creature desires to go. This should seem relatively fundamental. One does not run in panic in a random direction when one has the desire to go shopping. It is important to note that the laws governing fear movement are considerably more detailed than just getting the heck out of the fearful situation in a random direction. However, we will come to that a little later.

It would be impossible for me to describe the exact idiom that I am trying to convey in fear and desire up until this point.

It is important to note that when I refer to Numerical Epistemology, there is a lot more than straight numbers representing things. I fear that my critics may not read this section, and may already be furiously writing to me telling me how impossible my analysis is. The identity is constructed not just by individual numbers, but numbers that form maps and links. All of space is metaphorically carved out of the identity by the vision. From this carving process, the mind simplifies the edges over time. Grappling with the spatial reality (from this understanding of the spatial reality) goes on to produce deeper desires. This property of vision effecting identity is just one part of the identity but it is central to much of the dynamic formation. Thought, as shown through the ape's brain program, is a dynamic rounding, processing, simplification of the external world to try to come to some understanding. This is all beautifully rich, but cannot be described any deeper without resorting to a lot of mathematics. This, I am afraid, is the topic of the next chapter.

7. I See, Therefore I Am
(The Vision Paper)

'Befod, now we have found something to control the giant rabbit, it will stop eating our elderly...'
- Ic Productions ©1995 Tom Barbalet

Introduction

This document was written towards the end of February 1997 when the author was working for a company called Informed Sources writing intelligent database software. The information collected in this document was designed to be both a chapter in the Nervana simulation manual and a separate document. It was written in a period of very little sleep and external interaction. However, the thoughts offered are concise and the description reproducible and effective. Any glaring errors will be corrected by the author in future publications.

Equipment

In order to carry out the simple analysis of vision, all you will require is a tree with leaves and a bag of corn chips or some snack food with a sufficient crunch. These things will be needed to explain the way vision is constructed at high speeds. Now why are corn chips so crucial? The simple fact is that when one bites into a corn chip, one develops a certain tension in our jaw. When the grain of the chip breaks the eyes are moved a very small distance at high speeds. If one then stares at a the tree with leaves about four to eight meters way, while eating the corn chips you will notice the effects which I describe in the analysis of vision below.

Body

How do we see and what do we do with this information? Like many sections of this manual, I shall offer you a slow wander to my conclusion. If one was to take each ape and ask them to draw a map of what they saw the island to be like what would each of them draw? Is this not a fundamental part of the simulation? If the simulation could offer a solution to this problem, it may come a little closer to the big answers. Psychology, just primitive folk psychology offers us the correct answers. Areas the NA go to regularly should appear to be larger in their map of the island and sections of the island where they have never been should not appear, or perhaps as a rough guess. Some sections of the map where they have been infrequently should be erroneous as well, but how should it appear. Would sections be fuzzy? Would sections just be a good approximation of the reality? Let me ask one more abstract question. How does the NA in their facing in the x and y direction (i.e. along the land) develop an understanding of what the land looks like from above.

There are nearly no good road maps of Kuala Lumpur. I regularly walked distances and I had no idea of how big these areas were in any real mapping sense. If I had asked myself to draw a map from above I would have found that the distances for some streets did not match up and join. I also travelled in many different modes. I walked, I ran, I took taxis, I took the infamous KL minibuses, and I occasionally drove in private vehicles and each offered very new answers to my description of how far these distances really were. In Australia, I knew not just from experience but also through looking and trusting existing maps that I was traveling for so many kilometers, but intuitively when cycling for example, I found it hard to work out how far or how fast I had travelled. The NA have exactly the same problem. The way I combated my perspective problem in KL was to get on top a very tall building and actually look down on the city like it was a map of some sort. I then had an intimate feel of the streets and how they linked and how long they were through personally looking at them rather than trusting my own perspective on the ground or even worse a map!

Now one has constructed this notion of vision in words, how does one do it on a computer? This is really the cunning section of the application and it came to me in early February 1997 when I was setting up for a shed/studio warming party I was throwing in Canberra. I had an old 8080, 3 MHz thing, which could not do very much bar look old and green and dusty. I had a simple little point rounding algorithm that I used to use in my old polymorphic theory days when I had the esteemed title of 'Australia's last polymorphist' - the concept failed dismally and I continued to be single. Nevertheless, I found a number of ways of doing devious linear mathematics to achieve bizarre results.

I had been puzzling for quite some time about how the NA would think and how I could show this in a graphical way where people could say - 'Wow! I can see them thinking.' Moreover, previous AI-esque simulations had not offered very colorful or plausible link of the thoughts with the outside world. Robots looked at 400 screws in 1000 different positions and at the end of the information collection, the robot could recognize some number of times what was a screw and what wasn't before making an error - but no user could ask the program to describe a screw - the universal screw. So I was stuck, I needed to show the NA thinking in some form which was accessible to the user and actually showed what they were thinking about. This did not mean a Disney look into the NA minds with a large picture of a banana coming up.

I will now create an argument on how we see in stereo and a possible means of mapping stereo images in a simulation, with a little polymorphic theory thrown in for good measure.

Let us first begin by describing a static (non-moving) scene. Here represented by three forms. The circle represents a full moon; the upper zigzag, a mountain silhouette; and the lower shape the edge of a lake.

Image through the right eye

Image through the left eye

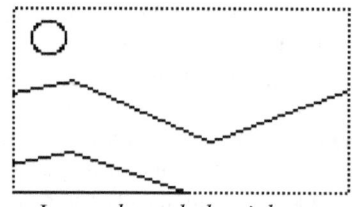

If the image were two-dimensional, it would be possible to line every object up perfectly when placing the two images next to one another. Nevertheless, as the image is three dimensional, when one lines one object up the remaining objects are not perfectly lined up.

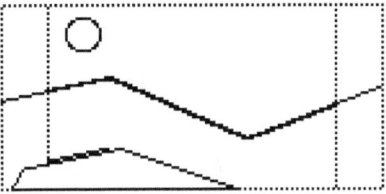

When one lines up the moon, for example, the mountains do not quite line up and the lake is noticeably unaligned.

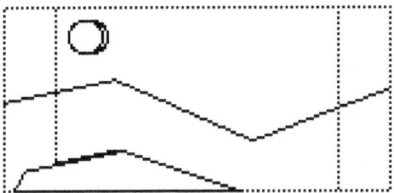

When one lines up the mountain, the moon is out slightly and the lake is out in the other direction.

When one lines up the lake, the moon is double and the mountains are poorly aligned.

This argument really proves nothing in terms of how is dimensionality achieved, but it does show that the only real information that our eyes give comes through two, two-dimensional images.

What we are doing when we slide the images over each other is a simple mathematical convolution. This would be a reasonable method for finding depth if there was a real way of distinguishing objects in the real world. It is easier to formulate an argument of depth, which does not rely on object justification, and this is why I will offer my polymorphic argument. Unfortunately, I had generated quite a successful argument about why the polymorphic method was so successful, but in

perfect time, my word processor crashed losing a large part of the document. I will try to reconcile my thoughts and pained emotions in order to explain the system again.
I shall begin with the diagram of the process.

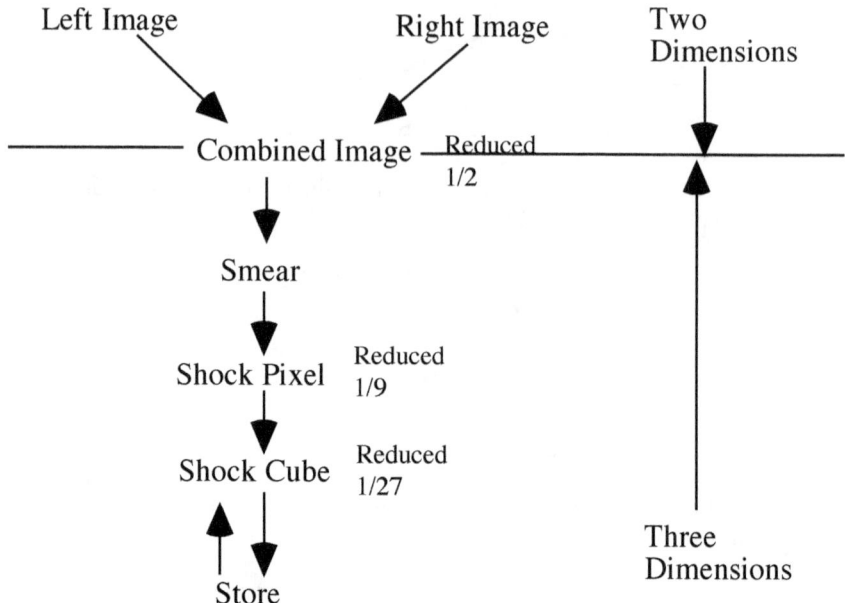

The left and the right images are overlaid on top of each other so they cover each other exactly. The information is placed into an array that develops the changes in color and hard lines as edges have the maximum value. Whereas the remainder has the minimum value. This reduces the two separate two-dimensional images to one two-dimensional image. This image is then smeared by a polymorphic method called the shock pixel method, here used both for smearing but also for reducing information.
One needs to imagine that there exists a point, a pixel, in the two dimensional image and surrounding it are other pixels. From here the surrounding pixels, plus the central pixel are added together and divided by the total number of pixels to offer an average value over the pixel space. To confuse matters a little more there is a shock pixel-div and a shock pixel-mod method that offers both the average but also the remainder form, but this should be expanded on in only some aspects of the polymorphic dimensionality argument. The only allowance that this makes is that the two-dimensional image can be reduced to pixels. When the image becomes deep and detailed enough this really should not be a problem as each individual pixel will be only about 1:10 000 the original image.

It is almost impossible to describe the effect of shock pixel smearing in a manual like this - purely because it is a graphical and a mathematical process that yields a ghostly abstract result. The description of dimensionality that results from the linked smearing between like shapes close to each other is a high numerical value. This surprisingly represents things that are far away from each other. Smaller results from similar shapes originally further apart in the overlay result in a concept of objects that are closer to the viewer. This again needs to be explained with a diagram.

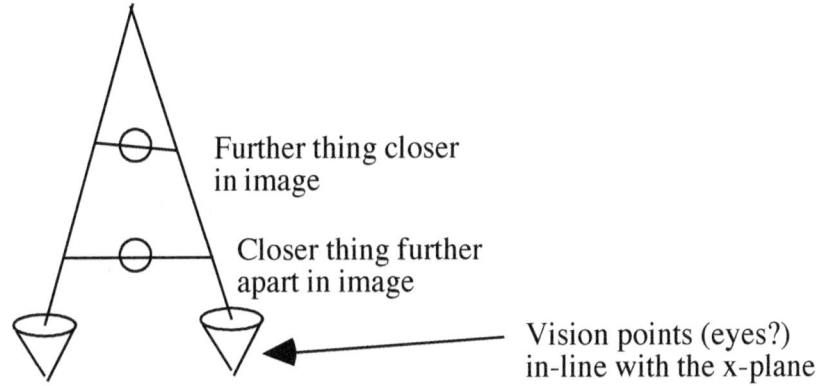

When the final points on the image are rounded, the points which are closer together will offer less blurring, that the points which are further apart. The more blurring then the smaller the value for the points surrounding the image-smears, then the lower the z-axis value. The lower the z-axis value then the closer to the observer.

Ideally, the difference between the edges and the non-edges that are fed into this smearing dimensionality argument would be very great. Let us say for example that the edge will equal 255 and the non-edge will equal 0.

This gives a full byte of depth information or 256 possible values for the z-axis. This information is particularly ridiculous because the depth of focus that we experience is without depth resolution. It should be noted that these 256 points are a very abstract quantity and do not tie into the real world.

It is also important to note that the more time the creature moves through the same area, the more the rounding develops larger values for the same locations and the bigger the space appears to be. Tying in with the psychology constructs developed previously.

Apart from the vision, the creature - the NA in this case - also moves through the space. Now this information is not collected but is outputted by the creature and is thus more controlled actually than the explanation of depth given by the vision information. The NA has an understanding of movement and a knowledge of movement that cannot be connected with their understanding or knowledge of the outside world.

Here we have to create a very interesting argument about the storage of visual information, and the building of a constructed reality. If you have been lost in the past six paragraphs, please at least try to understand this concept. We now have a planer map that is a value for z that is dependent on x and y. Thus, z has no real depth, but purely has dimensional information created from the smear and shock-pixel. Nevertheless, the NA's movement is externalized they have a x and y location as well as a direction facing.

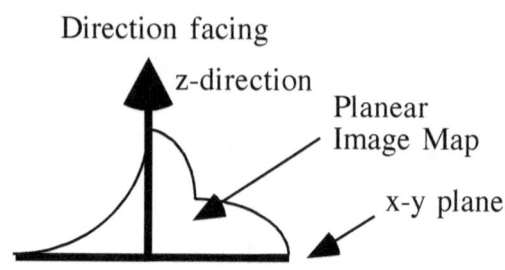

This diagram just shows the image map at one point (also simplified to one dimension, rather than two), but as the NA moves through space and their direction facing rotates, then many image maps are super positioned. This super positioning produces an aerial three-dimensional image that represents the commutation of information that the creature has collected about their surroundings. This image can be viewed as a three dimensional interactive interpretation of the reality that the creature believes exists. Technically the image could only ever be three dimensional through the vision input dimension + time (2 + 1 = 3 respectively!) But I would argue that the stereo two dimensional images smeared produces an extra 1/2 dimensions of interpreted depth and this is may be lost in the angular fixing which occurs when mapping the planer image to the movement space. There is a lot of extra dimensional information that cannot be described explicitly - like the motion through space and the rotational view. These add extra dimensional influences that enable the dimensionality argument to allow for the following;

2 d - both images through vision
1/2 d - interpreted z-axis (could really be anywhere between 0 and 1 d exclusive)
2 d - movement
1 d - rotation

Coming to a dimensionality of somewhere between five and six. This offers a vast depth of resolution of the universe. The only thing to do with this information is to store and compress it for future use. Here I will introduce the shock-cube that can really be of any dimension greater than two. The shock-cube functions like the shock-pixel in terms of rounding, but instead of that it takes it over 3^n compression where n is the number of dimensions.

The shock-cubed is applied to the information and then this is reapplied over time. This produces an understanding of the universe that is time dependent and thus explains memory degradation over time.

We have now defined enough information for the NA to describe what is on the island in a map form. Moreover, the map that they draw would be perfectly warped in terms of the larger, more familiar sections would connect to the less familiar sections. I have carefully avoided any of the mathematics involved in this system so I will spend a couple of paragraphs offering the math needed.

Firstly, I should begin by saying that vision and the resolution of vision is not really defined in terms of dots-per-unit or array based mechanics – it could be – but in order to make the system even more powerful we should assume that it may not be. This means that if it is, the system solves the solution and if it does not, the system is powerful enough to accurately model 'reality'.

$L(x, y)$ = the left eye image
$R(x, y)$ = the right eye image

$'L(x, y)$ = the right eye edge image (where $'L(x, y)=m$ if edge else $'L(x, y)=0$)

$'R(x, y)$ = the left eye edge image (where $'R(x, y)=m$ if edge else $'R(x, y)=0$)

$'L$ and $'R$ are mapped to V such that each infinite point of $'L$ equals the infinite point of $'R$

Effect 1

If a point is infinitely far from $'L$ and $'R$, then there exist only one point on V, but if a point is displayed close to $'L$ and $'R$ then there will be two points on V corresponding to the left and the right edge information.

Effect 2 (Specific to observers that only turn in the x-axis)

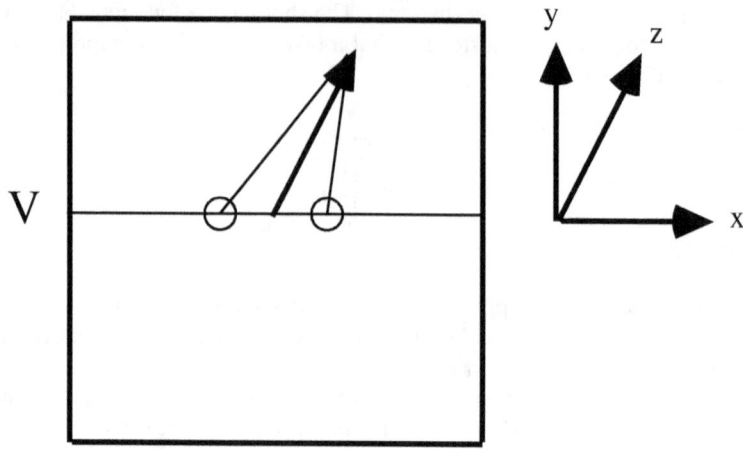

Linking y-points define 'objects'.

The definition of an object is really very abstract when you look at the basis of the system that we are dealing with the only shared points between a real object that is modeled in this system

This analysis offers a powerful method of describing passive movement through a static space but it does not offer any insight into motivation of movement. In order to find what we need to find remaining in the universe we need to construct a table of what we already know.

    Single position interpretation of static objects
    Movement through time and space leading to comprehension of static objects

These ideas can be described mathematically in terms of velocity (ds/dt).

8. Infinite vs. Identity

'I have come to a section of the simulation dealing with déjà vu and how to explain this phenomenon in a simulation sense. It also offers a really powerful insight into my analysis of situations. I will include it in a Chapter 8 of the Nervana manual dealing with perception and observation in advanced situations. This is really asking if the methods I employ in the simulation will ever be 'real' enough to simulate the complexity of day to day life in 'our' world.

How powerful can the simulation become? One needs to understand that the user approaches this chapter having read chapters 6 and 7 sequentially. Chapter 6 is a hand waving exercise where I describe my ideas of visual objects having emotional connectives and these emotional connectives are created through experience over time. Mathematically this to me is an integral effect over time in describing experience. Raw chemical emotions like fear are generated through a collection of objects, locations and times in a fast - no reflective - look-up table. A quickly accessible set of things that would create fear in the being. The direct movement effect of fear; wanting to get as far from the current location as possible i.e. when a creature has sufficient fear to warrant movement, they will panic (for want of a better term) and try to escape the location. It seems a little perverse that I have chosen to focus upon elements of the simulation such a fear and desire - and that I find these to be the constituent emotions. Desire is interesting too and I fear that I will need to define desire in order to complete the picture for those who have not read chapter 6 and 7. Desire is a complex rational for movement, for example, you have the desire to get a book by John Lennon from the library. The book is called 'Sky Writing By Word of Mouth'. In order to construct a notion of desire you need to ask the question; why do you want to go to the library to get that book - and here is my thought process;

        1)   I want to go to the library to get the book by Lennon
        2)   I read about the book, in another book, 'Let Me Take You Down' (about Lennon's murder)
        3)   I purchased 'Let Me Take You Down' because I feel a connection with Lennon's death and I needed something to read on a flight to Malaysia
        4)   I feel a connection with Lennon's death because I was young and impressionable at the time of his death and in a foreign country as well as the fact that I have listened to his musical all my life
        5)   I have listened to his music all my life because my parents had a large collection of his music
        6)   My parents had a large collection of his music because Lennon's music (and thought shown through his music) mostly agreed with their political beliefs

This is where the simulation breaks down slightly because desire as we encounter it in day to day ways is considerably more complex than in Nervana. Heaven forbid that the apes will one day want to go to libraries so they can get and read books about the ape Lennon and fly on planes and things of this nature. Nevertheless, as an author of a simulator I need to start to ask the questions of how complicated can the Nervana simulation get realistically. Ideally, the simulation could go on forever and we could live our whole lives watching these apes evolving over Planet Nervana!

As a digression, I create an argument that removes time from experience - this is good in a simulation sense because it means that if an ape repeats an action it does not need to remember every single time it did that action. For example, you go from home to work every day, you do not remember every time. However, more importantly and more subtly, if you were to return to the location of your home in ten years time having had that time away from your home and you were to repeat that action you would feel an effect of reminiscence physically. But I have found (perhaps only through myself as a being) that walking the same route that I did for eight or so years, after not seeing the family home in Deakin for a couple of years, made me believe for an instant that time did not exist and that I was still only a school boy returning from another day of school. Nevertheless, I quickly realized that it was not my home and that I was going to trespass if I walked any further!

My problem as I see it, is how much of the simulation - as it becomes more complex - will in fact be a detailed computer description of my own reality and not offer a real indication of the things I want to present. I am finding this quite concerning - as I am sure you would believe I could.'

I began work on Iota: Isle of the Apes (the simulation aspect of the project) just after I returned from Tasmania. It was important for me to work on this part of the project as it did not require any funding and it was also a place where a lot of interesting programming could be done. I had to introduce the Nervana Command-line Intelligent-interface (or NCI as it was known in the project). This in itself was a programming feat, but I also had to consider the two virtual reality engines I would have to employ. By far the most important task was to find names for the two VR engines. Those wacky ancient Greeks came to the rescue.

Psi - Continuous Infinite Engine

Phi - Fast-Fly-Over Infinite Engine

The Psi engine was designed for the ground-based, ape's eye view, virtual reality generation. This was primarily done in three modes;

    stationary
    walking
    running

These modes offer a decreasing degree of detail.

The Phi engine however is in constant motion both forwards over the tree tops as well as a lift and rotate. This regime offers an important insight into the structure of the virtual reality parameters that this engine would have. Ideally, there would exist only the following necessary specifications;

location x,y, z
velocity
facing x,y, z

These plus the island genetics would be passed to the program and the result would be a graphical image. Ideally, too, the location parameters would be remote within the program and the only accessed variables would be the change of facing and the velocity. There would also be an internal time parameter that would govern the moving of the ocean, the sunlight and things such as flocks of birds.

Having given a precursory glance at the two virtual reality engines within the simulation, I wish to ask a very important question. At what point should one optimize over the simulation of reality. This is a very real question because up until this point the desire mapping has been constructed as follows;

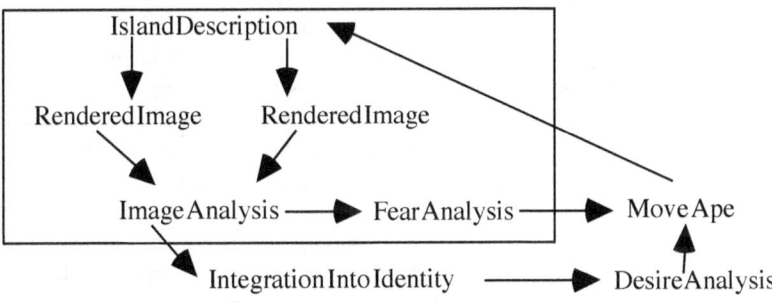

This needs to be done for each ape every allocated time delta which is currently a minute, but with effective programming should be returned to about three to five seconds (this is in SIMTIME and not REALTIME.) The parameter π is defined as;

π=REALTIME / SIMTIME

Ideally, π should be much greater than one. Prompting some kind of exploration of the NCI, typing **pi** will give the π value for the current computer and time in the simulation. As more new NA are born, the value for π will decrease.

Similarly, at night the value for π will increase dramatically. Back to the diagram above, the boxed area indicates a section of wheel reinvention. Ideally, the completely boxed section can be rewritten into a single function that can be passed to the Integration Into Identity section and to the Move Ape section. This relies on some philosophically valid approximation for the errors brought into the rendering of the stereo image and the visual interpretation algorithm.

I wish to offer some account of the subtle things that motivate learning. The subtle internal emotions that aid our identity and most importantly the way we move. This is a broad jump from the simulation perspective but of course, this analysis has important ramifications in the Nervana simulation that is now known as Iota.

The topic that I shall begin with is déjà vu. This is going to mean here, not the initial feeling that you have already been to a place where you have never in fact been before, but the sense that you are in a situation that you have already experienced. This is a crucial distinction, and alludes to the fact that I am actually substituting a word that has a different meaning for a word that does not exist to my knowledge.

It is the sense of déjà vu as described here that has motivated much of my life, and I think it is a must have explanation in a simulation such as this. Before I continue, I wish to return to the rabbits. I am doing this for two reasons. Firstly, I think it was important to note that I really do not care whether or not rabbits fall in love. Although this may shatter a few dreams of humanity resting with Barbalet, I merely brought up the rabbit point to lighten the academic load a little and also offer some indication to the kind of things that one should consider when one creates a simulation. Morally or perhaps more important, ethically I find many things that we take for granted in modern society are in fact strange manipulations of reality. I would say in reflection that the section of the manual that deals with rabbit love is a little self-indulgent and does not really make a clear point. It is however part of the manual that has been taken on with cult mythos and I have been told that I cannot edit that section of the manual on pain of? Who knows!

Let us return to the rabbits, to re indulge. Is it possible to see symptoms of déjà vu in the rabbit? Is it possible to put the rabbit in an identical situation or near identical and get the same reaction? My personal experience of déjà vu as I describe has always been to arouse fear and entice substantial change in my own existence. I think this kind of déjà vu is a subtle use of the fear operator, with a slight twist. What the fear operator does is it looks at the objects in front of the subject, this may also include abstract objects, such as location. In addition, it compares these objects with a set of fear causing objects and it then attributes a number representing fear and how much the observer wants to leave the situation. Déjà vu as described here is slightly different because the fear is created not by abstract previous experiences that burn the objects into the creatures fear list, but in fact, objects are added to the fear list after some reflection. These objects are not offered in abstract, e.g. fear of felines, fear of water etc. Nevertheless, as a complex linked class of objects that can be best represented by a sentence;

The ape, Basil, passing my mother some berries just before she ate them and fed them to my father and they both died.

This is a very crude description of a possible déjà vu situation, particularly if Basil either consciously or unconsciously has a habit of poisoning other apes, but also if after Basil's death due to a mysterious abseiling accident, other apes were observed passing on berries.

Can rabbits have similar déjà vu situations? Dogs certainly are known to have these kind of memory recognition of bad experiences, but when does this recognition occur? Does the dog go off and think to itself before it comes to the conclusion that the smell of antiseptic and the sounds of other dogs barking usually means a jabbing somewhere in their body? On the other hand, is there a time around recorder that looks at the events near-previous that have occurred. Thus if a bad experience happens the creature can say, 'Ah that is not just because of the berries, but also due to all the actions surrounding the berry experience.

9. Creation Information

Graham Wilson

This section of the manual would appear to be the least edited of all. This is because it deals with the people and the sounds of the Nervana application (even prior to the Nervana Project). I have tried to move the sentences into the past tense and introduce some discussion at the end about polymorphic sound. Although it is an uphill battle fighting my previous self.

The early part of the Nervana application and documentation was written heavily under the influence of 'Bring BACE (DMT FX-Yall Remix)'. The application specific sound 'Lucy In The Sky With Nervana' was described by effervescent DJ and close personal friend, Graham 'Tanooki' Wilson as 'a cat being strangled' - probably more a statement about the kind of friends I keep than the quality of the sound! I will include both sounds in my release of Nervana 0.5 as I doubt the BACE96 compiler will be ready by the end of this year. (As I have!)

Many users may wonder why there is not a zoom feature in the program, or at least a colorful animation of the NAs swaggering through the undergrowth. There are two prominent reasons for this, sex and violence. In the strangling cat conversation had with Graham, I commented that the application would no doubt gain notoriety if I added animations for when the felines attacked and killed an unsuspecting ape. Graham retorted, 'I think the you people would be far more interested in watching the apes getting it on.' There will not be an R-rated version of Nervana available until the simulation is operating to its full potential. (More than likely never!) [Although as an update to this information, a full R rated version will be the specifications for Nervana 0.5. Nervana 0.5 will come with a censored version that displays a map of England when any of the rude bits come up.]

The defining moment in this project came having watched the Simpsons' Halloween Special VI, the award winning Homer3. I found the whole episode unbelievably haunting. A moon landing equivalent of my generation. Seeing a two dimensional family or at least the father of a two dimensional family become a three dimensional entity in our world and the addition of the computer animation and the hex-code '4672696E6B2072756C657321' or 'Frink rules!' etched into the strange three dimensional universe (Frink being the nerdy-scientist). I found it hard to believe the addition of the two twelfth powers equate to the third twelfth power. To me this was what television should be, a whole lot of deep information, dressed up as entertainment.

Having now released the CD, or hopefully having gotten this text on the data part of the Nation of Nervana Isle of the Apes CD, I now can look back at the creation of tracks for the album. My efforts really came across the six months with the computer. The early tracks like Water in Creation and Drop on A Branch are merely thoughts of about 10-15 seconds put into sound. There is a lot of subtle parody on the album.

Favorite tracks for me? No. I really could not say. It is now 4.16AM on the morning the CD is to be pressed and I have only heard Bo Daley and the inSECT remixes for the first times yesterday. I shall offer no comment. I think both are equally different from my exploration. Although it should be noted, both use samples from the remaining tracks on the album. For all those trying to contact me by post, my email address is tom@nobleape.com.

The links between Nervana and my previous pieces of software may initially appear to be quite subtle. The link between an anti-viral program and a programming language, for example, come through the types of viruses the programs were designed to remove - namely polymorphic - Ic was a polymorphic compiler (not to be confused with a polymorphic virus compiler, which it certainly was not!). The link between the Dotman program was explained at the beginning of the manual. Vector 3 is the current virtual reality engine for the project.

Antiseptic had an intelligent command line interface that will be included in the final version of the program or perhaps a little sooner.

I was on the 'web on 6 March 1997 and I decided to do a search for the word 'Nervana' under the half dozen search engines that are offered. The problem is that there is some Ecstasy related term Nervana too - so I was in a Computational Physics lab and my search screen fills up with the Cloud 9/Ecstasy stuff and there through it was a couple of interesting points. The first was an Italian software site that had quite an impressive blurb - but unfortunately, I do not know Italian. It probably said something like - 'This Barbalet fellow is a real moron. He makes jokes that no one would understand and he pays us out just because he can't read the language.' And there was a US game site that listed 'Although you wouldn't guess it through the name, this application simulates apes on an island.' It always amazes me how something I create can keep people amused and the best part is that it is free.

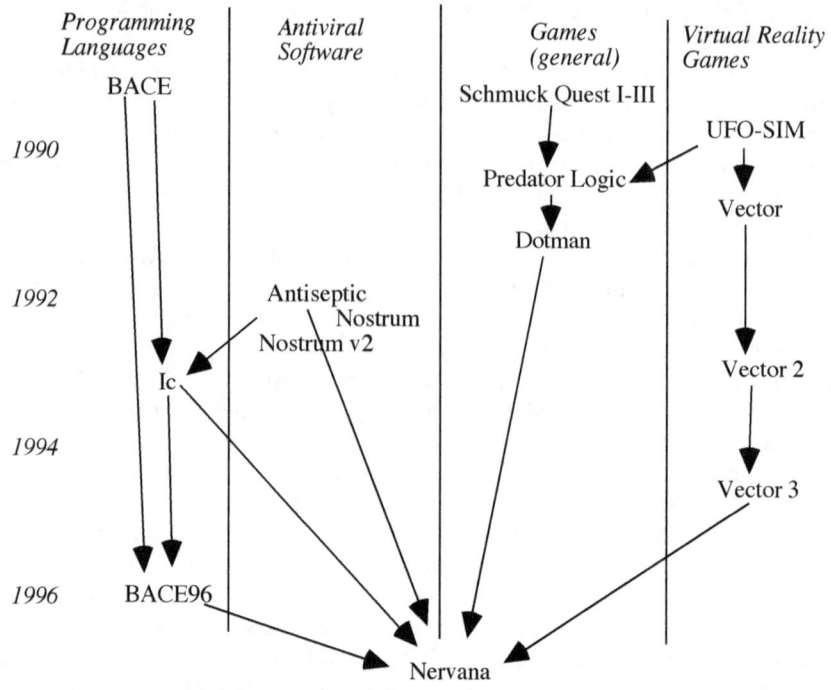

A Progression of Tom Barbalet's Software

The sense that someone in Italy would be using Nervana or at least would be offering it as a download for their own publicity is amazing.

1997 has been an interesting year thus far. I live the life of a hermit in this little shed about 800m from the centre of town and about 50m from my University. But I could go the whole day without saying more than ten words to another human. But I feel I should write comedy novels in this kind of sensory deprivation because my mind is exploding with concepts and ideas. The polymorphic math stuff is very interesting actually, because I am trying to find faster ways of doing the same calculations through simple group links.

On the morning of the final CD burn, I really feel there is nothing more to add. Too large a part of my existence has been Nervana. I had hoped I would receive some assistance with aspects of the programming and documentation. This has not been the case!

Appendix A - The Uniqueness of Nervana

Unfortunately mathematics offers us the uniqueness of the tree location with a little bit of theory. The idea goes something like this;

(1) There exists a tree and it exists on the z-direction of a three dimensional plane, coming from a surface z(x,y) (as previously described).

(2) This point also has a derivative vector description given by dz/dx and dz/dy.

(3) Take (1) and (2) and combine these three parameters in a matrix,
[z(x,y)   dz/dx(x,y)   dz/dy(x,y)]

(4) RTP

(x1)(x2)(y1)(y2)
  { [(x1◇x2)v(y1◇y2)] =>
    [(z(x1,y1)◇z(x2,y2)) v
    ((dz/dx(x1,y1)◇dz/dx(x2,y2)) v
    (dz/dy(x1,y1)◇dz/dy(x2,y2)))] }

In words, for all points (x,y) there exists no two points that have the same value for z, dz/dx or dz/dy.

The antecedent;

== (x1◇x2)v(y1◇y2)
== ~(x1=x2)v~(y1=y2)
== ~((x1=x2)&(y1=y2))

The consequent;

(z(x1,y1)◇z(x2,y2)) v
((dz/dx(x1,y1)◇dz/dx(x2,y2)) v
  (dz/dy(x1,y1)◇dz/dy(x2,y2)))

taking

== ((dz/dx(x1,y1)◇dz/dx(x2,y2)) v
  (dz/dy(x1,y1)◇dz/dy(x2,y2)))
== (~(dz/dx(x1,y1)=dz/dx(x2,y2)) v

~(dz/dy(x1,y1)=dz/dy(x2,y2)))
== ~((dz/dx(x1,y1)=dz/dx(x2,y2)) &
  (dz/dy(x1,y1)=dz/dy(x2,y2)))

taking

== (z(x1,y1)<>z(x2,y2))
== ~(z(x1,y1)=z(x2,y2))

by replacement, the consequent looks like this;

== ~(z(x1,y1)=z(x2,y2)) v
  ~((dz/dx(x1,y1)=dz/dx(x2,y2)) &
  (dz/dy(x1,y1)=dz/dy(x2,y2)))
== ~((z(x1,y1)=z(x2,y2)) &
  ((dz/dx(x1,y1)=dz/dx(x2,y2)) &
  (dz/dy(x1,y1)=dz/dy(x2,y2)))

Thus;

(x1)(x2)(y1)(y2)
  { [(x1<>x2)v(y1<>y2)] =>
    [(z(x1,y1)<>z(x2,y2)) v
    ((dz/dx(x1,y1)<>dz/dx(x2,y2)) v
    (dz/dy(x1,y1)<>dz/dy(x2,y2)))] }

becomes;

(x1)(x2)(y1)(y2)
  { [(z(x1,y1)=z(x2,y2)) &
    ((dz/dx(x1,y1)=dz/dx(x2,y2)) &
    (dz/dy(x1,y1)=dz/dy(x2,y2)))] =>
    [(x1=x2)&(y1=y2)] }

In words, for all points (x,y) if there are two points that have the same value for z, dz/dx or dz/dy, they are the same point.

Proof:

(Note: in order to prove this we will need to go back to the definition of z, dz/dx and dz/dy)

$$z(x,y) = ((f(x)/7)*(g(y)/7))/450 \qquad (1)$$

dz/dx(x,y) = ((df(x)/7)*(g(y)/7))/450   (2)
dz/dy(x,y) = ((f(x)/7)*(dg(y)/7))/450   (3)

z(x1,y1) = z(x2,y2)   (4) from (1)
f(x1)*g(y1) = f(x2)*g(y2)   (5) from (4)

dz/dx(x1,y1) = dz/dx(x2,y2)   (6) from (2)
df(x1)*g(y1) = df(x2)*g(y2)   (7) from (6)

dz/dy(x1,y1) = dz/dy(x2,y2)   (8) from (3)
f(x1)*dg(y1) = f(x2)*dg(y2)   (9) from (8)

Substituting this back into the logic formula;

(x1)(x2)(y1)(y2)
 { [(f(x1)*g(y1) = f(x2)*g(y2)) &
    ((df(x1)*g(y1) = df(x2)*g(y2)) &
     (f(x1)*dg(y1) = f(x2)*dg(y2)))] =>
    [(x1=x2)&(y1=y2)] }

Take the only case where the statement could be false. Consequent false, antecedent unknown.

(x1)(x2)(y1)(y2)
(x1<>x2) v (y1<>y2)
----
f(x1)*g(y1) = f(x2)*g(y2)
df(x1)*g(y1) = df(x2)*g(y2)
f(x1)*dg(y1) = f(x2)*dg(y2)

Now over the section 0 to pi there exists only one point with the vector [sin x cos x]. This is due to the linear independence over this interval of sine and cosine. From this premise one can construct a vector which represents a sine equation (i.e. sin x + sin 2x/a) and a cosine equation based on its derivative which are linearly independent over the interval 0 to pi. Thus if two points from 0 to pi (inclusive) are taken and the described vectors are equal then the points are the same.

If we apply the fact that this cannot be true for the case. Thus;

f(x1)<>f(x2)
df(x1)<>df(x2)
g(y1)<>g(y2)
dg(y1)<>dg(y2)

Or more importantly;

$f(x1)/f(x2) \diamond 1$
$df(x1)/df(x2) \diamond 1$
$g(y1)/g(y2) \diamond 1$
$dg(y1)/dg(y2) \diamond 1$

Now with these cases we need to prove that all of these;

$f(x1)*g(y1) = f(x2)*g(y2)$
$df(x1)*g(y1) = df(x2)*g(y2)$
$f(x1)*dg(y1) = f(x2)*dg(y2)$

can remain true.

$f(x1)/f(x2) = g(y2)/g(y1) = r$ (1)
$r \diamond 1$

$g(y1)/g(y2) = df(x2)/df(x1) = 1/r$ (2)

$f(x1)/f(x2) = dg(y2)/dg(y1) = 1/r$ (3)

from (2) and (3),
$g(y1)/g(y2) = f(x1)/f(x2) = 1/r$ (4)

but through (1),
$f(x1)/f(x2) = r$ (5)

thus through (4) and (5),
$r = 1/r$

which can only be the case if r=1 or r=-1. But over the limiting range from 0 to pi the case of r=-1 is impossible. Thus r=1. Therefore, the antecedent of the claim is false when the consequent is false, and thus there can only exist true cases of;

$(x1)(x2)(y1)(y2)$
   $\{ [(f(x1)*g(y1) = f(x2)*g(y2)) \&$
     $((df(x1)*g(y1) = df(x2)*g(y2)) \&$
       $(f(x1)*dg(y1) = f(x2)*dg(y2)))] =>$
   $[(x1=x2) \& (y1=y2)] \}$

which through logical equality also proves;

(x1)(x2)(y1)(y2)
  { [(x1<>x2)v(y1<>y2)] =>
   [(z(x1,y1)<>z(x2,y2)) v
    ((dz/dx(x1,y1)<>dz/dx(x2,y2)) v
     (dz/dy(x1,y1)<>dz/dy(x2,y2)))] }

(where x1,x2,y1,y2 are over the range 0 to pi and f and g and df and dg are defined as given above). Having done all of this, no seeing creature can recognize a height. But fortunately, the true equation remains true even if the height factor is removed. Also dz/dx and dz/dy are dependent on the creature's perception of the x and y axis. One can see that by multiplying the dz/dx by a cosine factor and the dz/dy by a sine factor will in fact not change its inequality in any way and thus the result still holds with a change in perspective of the given axis. But this is not in fact what we are trying to say. If I can change my logic form a bit the real outcome desired is;

(x1)(x2)(y1)(y2)(a1)(a2)
(cos a1)*f(x1)*(sin a1)*g(y1) = (cos a2)*f(x2)*(sin a2)*g(y2)
(cos a1)*df(x1)*(sin a1)*g(y1) = (cos a2)*df(x2)*(sin a2)*g(y2)
(cos a1)*f(x1)*(sin a1)*dg(y1) = (cos a2)*f(x2)*(sin a2)*dg(y2)

(x1=x2)&(y1=y2)

Intuitively this can only be the case if;

f(x)<>g(x)
df(x)<>dg(x)

i.e. as long as the x axis does not equal the y axis. Now we must harp back to the question, why are we considering the uniqueness of points and their derivatives. Or more importantly why are we considering the uniqueness of the point's derivatives? What does this do in the simulation?

Appendix B - Polymorphic Image Analysis

The concept of the shock pixel or the smear is so central to the analysis of dimensionality developed in the Nervana Project. I have decided to offer an appendix in order to describe the mathematics behind the process. Sadly, there exists no reliable text on the fundamentals of polymorphic thought. Although I have a large file called Practical Polymorphism that acts as my own personal notebook for bits and pieces I have collected over the ages. The important notation is based on my Ic standard (or perhaps that should be BACEd?) Very simply there exists a 2d array which we shall call A. I shall write this all in BASIC notation initially as it is the most fundamental language. I normally program in C and will offer C improvements to the algorithm.

```
defint a-z
dim a(1,100,100)
gosub find
b&=0
while b&<>(99*99)
gosub smear
wend
gosub display
end

smear:
        for x=1 to 99
                for y=1 to 99
                        d&=0
                        for tx=-1 to 1
                                for ty=-1 to 1
                                        d&=d&+a(0,x+tx,y+ty)
                                next
                        next
                        if (a(1,x,y)=d&/9) then b&=b&+1
                        a(1,x,y)=d&/9
                next
        next
        for x=1 to 99
                for y=1 to 99
                        a(0,x,y)=a(1,x,y)
                next
        next
return
```

```
find:
        for x=0 to 100
                for y=0 to 100
                        a(0,x,y)=0
                next
        next
return

display:
return
```

This image panel comes from the original manual (hence the English/Australian spelling.)

This simple smear until static process described what shock-pixeling does. It is almost identical to aperture effects in optics. Through this notion of static, it appears that a pixel is a shock pixel if and only if [p'(x,y)] = [p(x,y) + p(x-1,y) + p(x-1,y-1) + p(x+1,y) + p(x+1,y+1) + p(x,y+1) + p(x-1,y+1) + p(x+1,y-1) / 9]

Appendix C - There Exists A Tree: Everything There Is To Know About Infinite Virtual Reality in Non-Mathematical Language

When one uses the Nervana application, a term that is regularly used is infinite virtual reality. Now many will ask what exactly is infinite virtual reality and what can it be used for? It can be explained through a simple thought argument.

Firstly, it should be acknowledged that there is something special about our understanding of our own existence. Each of us has a belief - at least most of the time - that we actually exist. This is a pretty powerful thought to have, even though we take it for granted.

Let us imagine a maze where each turn in the maze looks exactly the same as the previous turn in the maze. This is physically impossible in reality, but we should imagine that such a place might be possible. Perhaps an ancient civilization could have used it as a torture. So this maze exists and in the maze is placed a child. This child grows up in the maze. Now we should ask what kind of understanding does that child have of their own existence. This is an important question and it can be likened to what happens to cavers that are left for only small amounts of time (around two hours) in pitch-black caves. In such situations, the understanding of self existence breaks down very quickly.

The Nervana application is trying to create an existence for the Noble Apes that inhabit the simulated island. It is important that each point on the island is unique - that is that the NA cannot see exactly the same thing on two points of the island. This really tests the powers of the infinite virtual reality process.

But I have not begun to discuss infinite virtual reality yet. Before we can begin to do this, we need to consider that there exists a tree somewhere on the island. Now where would be the best place for this tree to exist? A tree cannot exist in a whole series of places. A tree cannot exist where there is sea-water. A tree cannot exist on the same point as a rock. But where can sea-water exist? Sea-water can exist at certain points where the land is below sea-level. A rock exists in places where the slope is not too great. Now a tree cannot exist where there is no sunlight - or more importantly, where there is never any sunlight. So there are some important parameters for this tree and they are;

    slope
    height
    sunlight
    sea-water

We have introduced another concept to do with sunlight, for there are creatures on the island that do not like sunlight - mice for example dislike sunlight. But this sunlight is moving sunlight and not the total sunlight. So let us add;

moving sunlight

Now all this really comes from the shape of the island or the height (and the slope that is really connected to the height).

Now if we look at every point on the island, which is different mathematically (this comes from Appendix A; so you will have to believe this with a little blind faith), we can play the little game of 'does there exist a tree here?' or perhaps 'does there exist a fish here?' or does there exist a night bird here?'. And this gives some idea of how infinite virtual reality works.

www.ingramcontent.com/pod-product-compliance
Lightning Source LLC
Chambersburg PA
CBHW072230170526
45158CB00002BA/837